PENGUIN BOOKS

BRIGHT STAR

JOHN KEATS was born in October 1795, son of the manager of a livery stable in Moorfields. His father died in 1804 and his mother, of tuberculosis, in 1810. By then he had received a good education at John Clarke's Enfield private school. In 1811 he was apprenticed to a surgeon, completing his professional training at Guy's Hospital in 1816. His decision to commit himself to poetry rather than a medical career was a courageous one, based more on a challenge to himself than any actual achievement.

His genius was recognized and encouraged by early friends such as Charles Cowden Clarke and J. H. Reynolds, and in October 1816 he met Leigh Hunt, whose *Examiner* had already published Keats's first poem. Only seven months later *Poems* (1817) appeared. Despite the high hopes of the Hunt circle, it was a failure. By the time *Endymion* was published in 1818 Keats's name had been identified with Hunt's 'Cockney School', and the Tory *Blackwood's Magazine* delivered a violent attack on Keats as a lower-class vulgarian, with no right to aspire to 'poetry'.

But for Keats fame lay not in contemporary literary politics but with posterity. Spenser, Shakespeare, Milton and Wordsworth were his inspiration and challenge. The extraordinary speed with which Keats matured is evident from his letters. In 1818 he had worked on the powerful epic fragment *Hyperion*, and in 1819 he wrote 'The Eve of St Agnes', 'La Belle Dame sans Merci', the major odes, *Lamia*, and the deeply exploratory *Fall of Hyperion*. Keats was already unwell when preparing the 1820 volume for the press; by the time it appeared in July he was desperately ill. He died in Rome in 1821.

Keats's final volume did receive some contemporary critical recognition, but it was not until the latter part of the nineteenth century that his place in English Romanticism began to be recognized, and not until the twentieth century that it became fully recognized.

JANE CAMPION was born in Wellington, New Zealand in 1954. Her parents, Edith and Richard Campion, studied theatre at RADA and later formed the New Zealand Players with the idea of touring professional theatre throughout the country. Later they turned to farming on a mixed sheep and cattle property that ran from the main road north to the beach at Peka Peka.

Jane Campion studied Anthropology at Victoria University in Wellington and painting at both Chelsea School of Arts in London and Sydney College of Arts. While at the Australian Film, Television and Radio School she completed three short films, *Peel*, *A Girl's Own Story* and *Passionless Moments* co-authored with Gerard Lee. *Peel* won the Palme d'Or at Cannes. *Sweetie*, co-written by Gerard Lee, was her first feature film, followed by *An Angel at My Table* and *The Piano*, which won the Palme d'Or at the 1993 Cannes Film Festival, as well as eight Oscar nominations and three Oscars including Best Screenplay for Jane Campion in 1994. Subsequent films were *Portrait of a Lady*, *Holy Smoke* (co-written with Anna Campion and currently being adapted for the stage) and *In the Cut*.

Bright Star is the first film following Jane Campion's four year break from 2003–2007 and has been written by her from an original idea. She is currently in development with 2B Films, Pathé and Screen Australia to make *Runaway*, an adaptation of an Alice Munro story.

JOHN KEATS

✳

Bright Star

Love Letters and Poems
of John Keats to Fanny Brawne

PENGUIN BOOKS

PENGUIN BOOKS

Published by the Penguin Group
Penguin Group (USA) Inc., 375 Hudson Street,
New York, New York 10014, U.S.A.
Penguin Group (Canada), 90 Eglinton Avenue East, Suite 700, Toronto,
Ontario, Canada M4P 2Y3 (a division of Pearson Penguin Canada Inc.)
Penguin Books Ltd, 80 Strand, London WC2R 0RL, England
Penguin Ireland, 25 St Stephen's Green, Dublin 2, Ireland
(a division of Penguin Books Ltd)
Penguin Group (Australia), 250 Camberwell Road, Camberwell,
Victoria 3124, Australia (a division of Pearson Australia Group Pty Ltd)
Penguin Books India Pvt Ltd, 11 Community Centre,
Panchsheel Park, New Delhi – 110 017, India
Penguin Group (NZ), 67 Apollo Drive, Rosedale, North Shore 0632,
New Zealand (a division of Pearson New Zealand Ltd)
Penguin Books (South Africa) (Pty) Ltd, 24 Sturdee Avenue,
Rosebank, Johannesburg 2196, South Africa

Penguin Books Ltd, Registered Offices:
80 Strand, London WC2R 0RL, England

First published in Penguin Books (UK) and Penguin Books (USA) 2009

1 3 5 7 9 10 8 6 4 2

Selection copyright © Penguin Books Ltd. 2009
Introduction copyright © Jane Campion, 2009
All rights reserved

ISBN 978-0-14-311774-2
CIP data available

Printed in the United States of America

Contents

Introduction

Bright Star – The Story of Keats and Fanny

When twenty-three-year-old John Keats met eighteen-year-old Fanny Brawne in the autumn of 1818, a love affair began, and the thirty-seven surviving love letters and notes Keats wrote to Fanny, as well as the poems collected in this book, bear compelling witness to its tenderness, passion and intensity. It was the first love most of us dream of enjoying, but with an end so tragic that it proved hard for them to bear.

To the wider world and even to his brother, Keats maintained a self-mocking distance on the subject of romance. So, when he first met Fanny Brawne, he worked as hard to disguise his interest as he did to enjoy it. 'Shall I give you Miss Brawn[e]?' he wrote to his brother and sister in-law in December. He went on:

> She is about my height – with a fine style of countenance of the lengthen'd sort – she wants sentiment in every feature – she manages to make her hair look well – her nostrils are fine – though a little painful . . . but she is ignorant – monstrous in her behaviour, flying out in all directions . . . I was forced lately to make use of the term *Minx* – this is I think not from any innate vice, but from a penchant she has for acting stylishly – I am however tired of such style and shall decline any more of it.

Keats had just met the great love of his life, but neither he nor she knew it. Reading this extract from his letter it is easy to feel the energy, the relaxed relish with which he imposed a cool, yet playful eye over Miss Brawne. She had got under his guard.

In Hampstead, the young girl was famous both for her attention to fashion as well as for her *bons mots*. Her uncle was the dandy of the day, Beau Brummell, and he may well have tutored his niece's obsession with clothes. She was described by a contemporary as everything that is meant by the word 'unusual' and she, like Keats, was only five foot tall.

Keats had met his petite equal, lippy and combative, and within a year, he would be writing of her in quite another way.

> Pillowed upon my fair love's ripening breast,
>   To feel for ever its soft swell and fall
> Awake forever in a sweet unrest,
>   Still, still to hear her tender-taken breath

What had happened? Keats had fallen completely in love. The early part of the affair has few markers. He barely ever mentioned her again in any letters to either his brother or sister, and he did not write to Fanny either. He didn't need to, as Fanny Brawne and Keats both lived in Hampstead and were part of a small tight circle. Mrs Brawne, a widow, was well liked and popular with Keats's best friend, Charles Brown, as well as with the Dilkes family with whom Brown shared the house, which then was divided into two separate living quarters. Sometime in the spring of 1819, the Brawne family took over the Dilkes' half of the property and Fanny and Keats began living in the same house, sharing the same garden and, most likely, many meals as well.

During this spring Keats famously experienced the great outpouring of his poetic life. He completed 'The Eve of St Agnes', 'La Belle Dame sans Merci', 'Ode to Psyche', 'Ode on a Grecian Urn', 'Ode to a Nightingale', 'Ode on Melancholy' and 'Ode on Indolence'.

Other factors also contributed to this period of creativity. Keats's younger brother Tom had died the previous December. He was nineteen years old. Keats had nursed him as he coughed blood and became increasingly weak and miserable. There was no one else to help; their parents were both dead and Keats's brother George and his wife had emigrated to America. Keats had recovered from the worst of the grief and now had a period of time when he could write. Brown had insisted on Keats staying with him, alleviating Keats's financial worries. His health was for once good, spring had begun and he was falling in love.

Fanny and Keats became close in these very unusual circumstances. Both of them would have recognized how extremely financially unacceptable marriage would be between them, yet with the constant ease of access and little thought for the future, the young couple enjoyed many opportunities for 'tiffing and making up'. Good-natured Mrs Brawne had little reason to be suspicious. Fanny was as interested as her mother in marrying well and she did not like poetry, preferring trumpery novels and politics. Keats's friend Brown thought otherwise; he noticed Keats's growing attachment and many times pointed out the potential dangers to his career should Fanny entrap him. He did not believe Fanny was in any way Keats's equal.

In the early summer of 1819, Brown and Keats left Hampstead for an extended writing retreat on the Isle of Wight. Brown rented out his half of the Hampstead house to raise money. Keats and Fanny were separated. The first letter to Fanny arrives a week later. Reading the letter today one feels it shockingly present, like a handhold or a kiss, *his exact words as he wrote them and she read them, and re-read them, kept and treasured them her whole life*:

Ask yourself my love whether you are not very cruel to have so entrammeled me, so destroyed my freedom . . . I almost wish we were butterflies and liv'd but three summer days – three such days with you I could fill with more delight than fifty common years could ever contain.

In this letter and the ones that followed, Keats poured out his heart. He was self-mocking, pleading, vulnerable, jealous, funny, tender and stunningly truthful.

Fanny was so affected by Keats's departure that she became literally love sick. By the middle of summer, the realities of their situation had sunk in. Keats had neither the money nor the promise of money on which to marry. His first book of poetry had sold poorly and earned famously cruel reviews. Then after a month of not writing, he wrote dispiritedly, admitting that he was 'endeavouring to wean' himself from her.

When Brown returned to Wentworth Place in Hampstead and the Brawnes, Keats did not join him. He intended to find rooms in Westminster near to the Dilkes and away from Fanny. The resolve did not last. When Keats and Fanny re-met shortly after, the love between them had not diminished with distance but deepened. In mid October, he writes, 'I cannot exist without you. I am forgetful of everything but seeing you again . . . You have absorb'd me. I have a sensation at the present moment as though I was dissolving.' Shortly after he adds, 'On awakening from my three days dream . . . I should like to cast the die for Love or death. I have no patience with any thing else.' Keats moved back to live next door in Hampstead. He gave Fanny his mother's garnet ring and while the young couple believed themselves engaged, Mrs Brawne and their friends strenuously protested. But the couple grew closer still. Keats prepared his next book of poems in the hope that it would be successful enough so they could finally marry. Whenever Keats and Fanny were alone she wore his ring on her engagement finger, and when in company on her middle finger.

In February 1820, Keats went into town without his

greatcoat and returned late, cold and feverish. He staggered so badly that Brown thought him drunk. As he got into bed he coughed slightly, and seeing a single drop of blood upon the sheet said to Brown, 'I know the colour of that blood; – it is arterial blood . . . that drop of blood is my death-warrant.' Later that night, a large lung haemorrhage followed that almost suffocated him. All he could think of was Fanny. Keats's doctor believed love frustration was a contributing factor. For the sake of his health, Keats was kept away from Fanny, and Brown, who was still criticizing her, was zealous in maintaining their separation. They communicated by notes and Fanny 'showing herself in the garden' while Keats convalesced on a daybed inside. 'I think you had better not make any long stay with me when Mr. Brown is at home. Whenever he goes out you may bring your work,' Keats wrote her in a note.

At first, Keats was hopeful of a full recovery, but after a long convalescence and repeated haemorrhages, he began to despair. His letters and notes to Fanny, so often playful and loving, became cloying and paranoid. To make things worse, Brown's financial circumstances were severely reduced, forcing Keats to live elsewhere. Brown had been conducting a romance of his own with the maid and she was pregnant. All Keats's doctors believed that his only chance for life would be to leave England for Italy before the winter. Fanny desperately wanted to travel with him but it was impossible. In the last month of his time in England, ill and disturbed, a feverish Keats made his way back to Wentworth Place, and Mrs Brawne took pity and allowed him to stay. He remained with the Brawnes until he left England for Rome.

Mrs Brawne accepted that Keats and Fanny had become engaged and promised that when Keats returned the following spring they could marry and he could live with them. She had been won over and may also have thought any return highly unlikely. The Brawnes fed and cared for

Keats and delighted in his company. As the day of his departure for Italy arrived, it felt to Fanny unbearable and unreal. Keats himself reports that she asked repeatedly, 'Is there another life? . . . There must be, we cannot be created for this kind of suffering.' The couple separated at the Pond Street Depot in Hampstead. Keats's friend Leigh Hunt, who was with him, commented later on their outward composure while 'neither of them entertained a hope to see each other again in life'.

Keats did not write to Fanny again. He could not bear it. Instead he wrote to Brown, 'I can bear to die – I cannot bear to leave her . . . My dear Brown, what am I to do? Where can I look for consolation or ease? If I had any chance of recovery, this passion would kill me.'

The last letters of Keats to his friend Brown make almost unbearable reading. He was tormented by visions of Fanny and fears of his approaching death that would separate them for ever. Fanny's letters to Keats have not survived, the ones she wrote to him in Italy were buried with him, unopened.

When Fanny was told of Keats's death, the effect on her was terrible. The twenty-year-old cut her hair short and spent three years in widow's black, roaming the paths on the Heath where she and Keats had walked together.

Fanny did not marry until she was thirty-three; she then had three children and lived into old age. Her letters from Keats were released fifteen years after her death and, by some, were considered an outrage. Keats was harshly criticized for being unmanly and improper. The letters were never, of course, meant to be read by anyone but Fanny. It is staggering to re-read them and share their intimacy and the uncensored honesty with which Keats so fully exposed himself to his young lover. The love affair had knocked Keats sideways. The young man, who two years earlier laughed at love, had been transformed. Now Keats could write about love with the only authority he ever accepted, that of experience itself. Keats surrendered himself utterly to Fanny; together they were soulmates and, on this earth, inseparable. Imaginatively they wove an intricate love web about themselves, disapproved of by their friends but reinforced by their mutual attraction and sensitivity.

For Keats, despite his wretched pain in missing Fanny, it is impossible to wish his love had been milder. Keats died at twenty-five, more beloved on earth than most of us will ever be.

The poems, the letters, the love story are all part of the alchemy that makes Keats so special, so available to successive generations of readers. The young man who died devastated, convinced that he would be forgotten, has been repeatedly re-discovered. For many people, he is the first point of entry into poetry and his life story is a big part of that magical equation.

Eight years ago, I was drawn into Keats's world by Andrew Motion's moving biography. Soon I was reading back and forth between Keats's letters and his poems. The letters were fresh, intimate and irreverent, as though he was present and speaking. They were also intense with his own philosophy, such as 'The vale of Soulmaking', or 'Negative Capability'. The Keats spell went very deep for me. I finally wrote a screenplay of the love affair from Fanny's point of view, entitled *Bright Star*. I met Andrew Motion and even a great-great-great-granddaughter of Fanny. Last year, *Bright Star* was made into a feature film that has just been completed.

Thank you Keats, thank you Fanny. Rest in peace. 'Tender is the night.'

Jane Campion, May 2009

Letters of John Keats
to Fanny Brawne

by Joseph Severn 28 Jan.y 1821, 3 O'Clock morn.g

My dearest Fanny,

I–IX.
SHANKLIN, WINCHESTER, WESTMINSTER.

I.

Shanklin,
Isle of Wight, Thursday.
[*Postmark*, Newport, 3 July, 1819.]

My dearest Lady,

I am glad I had not an opportunity of sending off a Letter which I wrote for you on Tuesday night – 'twas too much like one out of Rousseau's Heloise. I am more reasonable this morning. The morning is the only proper time for me to write to a beautiful Girl whom I love so much: for at night, when the lonely day has closed, and the lonely, silent, unmusical Chamber is waiting to receive me as into a Sepulchre, then believe me my passion gets entirely the sway, then I would not have you see those Rhapsodies which I once thought it impossible I should ever give way to, and which I have often laughed at in another, for fear you should [think me] either too unhappy or perhaps a little mad. I am now at a very pleasant Cottage window, looking onto a beautiful hilly country, with a glimpse of the sea; the morning is very fine. I do not know how elastic my spirit might be, what pleasure I might have in living here and breathing and wandering as free as a stag about this beautiful Coast if the remembrance of you did not weigh so upon me. I have never known any unalloy'd Happiness for many days together: the death or sickness of some one has always spoilt my hours – and now when none such troubles oppress me, it is you must confess very hard that another sort of pain should haunt me. Ask yourself my love whether you are not very cruel to have so entrammelled me, so destroyed my freedom. Will you confess this in the Letter you must write immediately and do all you can to console me in it – make it rich as a draught of poppies to intoxicate me – write the softest words and kiss them that I may at least touch my lips where yours have been. For myself I know not how to express my devotion to so fair a form: I want a brighter word than bright, a fairer word than fair. I almost wish we were butterflies and liv'd but three summer days – three such days with you I could fill with more delight than fifty common years could ever contain. But however selfish I may feel, I am sure I could never act selfishly: as I told you a day or two before I left Hampstead, I will never return to London if my Fate does not turn up Pam or at least a Court-card. Though I could centre my Happiness in you, I cannot expect to engross your heart so entirely – indeed if I thought you felt as much for me as I do for you at this moment I do not think I could restrain myself from seeing you again tomorrow for the delight of one embrace. But no – I must live upon hope and Chance. In case of the worst that can happen, I shall still love you – but what hatred shall I have for another! Some lines I read the other day are continually ringing a peal in my ears:

> To see those eyes I prize above mine own
> Dart favors on another –
> And those sweet lips (yielding immortal nectar)
> Be gently press'd by any but myself –
> Think, think Francesca, what a cursed thing
> It were beyond expression!

J.

Do write immediately. There is no Post from this Place, so you must address Post Office, Newport, Isle of Wight. I know before night I shall curse myself for having sent you so cold a Letter; yet it is better to do it as much in my senses as possible. Be as kind as the distance will permit to your

J. KEATS.

Present my Compliments to your mother, my love to Margaret and best remembrances to your Brother – if you please so.

II.

July 8th.
[*Postmark*, Newport, 10 July, 1819.]

My sweet Girl,

Your Letter gave me more delight than any thing in the world but yourself could do; indeed I am almost astonished that any absent one should have that luxurious power over my senses which I feel. Even when I am not thinking of you I receive your influence and a tenderer nature stealing upon me. All my thoughts, my unhappiest days and nights, have I find not at all cured me of my love of Beauty, but made it so intense that I am miserable that you are not with me: or rather breathe in that dull sort of patience that cannot be called Life. I never knew before, what such a love as you have made me feel, was; I did not believe in it; my Fancy was afraid of it, lest it should burn me up. But if you will fully love me, though there may be some fire, 'twill not be more than we can bear when moistened and bedewed with Pleasures. You mention 'horrid people' and ask me whether it depend upon them whether I see you again. Do understand me, my love, in this. I have so much of you in my heart that I must turn Mentor when I see a chance of harm befalling you. I would never see any thing but Pleasure in your eyes, love on your lips, and

6

Happiness in your steps. I would wish to see you among those amusements suitable to your inclinations and spirits; so that our loves might be a delight in the midst of Pleasures agreeable enough, rather than a resource from vexations and cares. But I doubt much, in case of the worst, whether I shall be philosopher enough to follow my own Lessons: if I saw my resolution give you a pain I could not. Why may I not speak of your Beauty, since without that I could never have lov'd you? – I cannot conceive any beginning of such love as I have for you but Beauty. There may be a sort of love for which, without the least sneer at it, I have the highest respect and can admire it in others: but it has not the richness, the bloom, the full form, the enchantment of love after my own heart. So let me speak of your Beauty, though to my own endangering; if you could be so cruel to me as to try elsewhere its Power. You say you are afraid I shall think you do not love me – in saying this you make me ache the more to be near you. I am at the diligent use of my faculties here, I do not pass a day without sprawling some blank verse or tagging some rhymes; and here I must confess, that (since I am on that subject) I love you the more in that I believe you have liked me for my own sake and for nothing else. I have met with women whom I really think would like to be married to a Poem and to be given away by a Novel. I have seen your Comet, and only wish it was a sign that poor Rice would get well whose illness makes him rather a melancholy companion: and the more so as so to conquer his feelings and hide them from me, with a forc'd Pun.

I kiss'd your writing over in the hope you had indulg'd me by leaving a trace of honey. What was your dream? Tell it me and I will tell you the interpretation thereof.

Ever yours, my love!

JOHN KEATS.

Do not accuse me of delay – we have not here an opportunity of sending letters every day. Write speedily.

III.

Sunday Night.

[*Postmark*, 27 July, 1819.]

My sweet Girl,

     I hope you did not blame me much for not obeying your request of a Letter on Saturday: we have had four in our small room playing at cards night and morning leaving me no undisturb'd opportunity to write. Now Rice and Martin are gone I am at liberty. Brown to my sorrow confirms the account you give of your ill health. You cannot conceive how I ache to be with you: how I would die for one hour – for what is in the world? I say you cannot conceive; it is impossible you should look with such eyes upon me as I have upon you: it cannot be. Forgive me if I wander a little this evening, for I have been all day employ'd in a very abstract Poem and I am in deep love with you – two things which must excuse me. I have, believe me, not been an age in letting you take possession of me; the very first week I knew you I wrote myself your vassal; but burnt the Letter as the very next time I saw you I thought you manifested some dislike to me. If you should ever feel for Man at the first sight what I did for you, I am lost. Yet I should not quarrel with you, but hate myself if such a thing were to happen – only I should burst if the thing were not as fine as a Man as you are as a Woman. Perhaps I am too vehement, then fancy me on my knees, especially when I mention a part of your Letter which hurt me; you say speaking of Mr. Severn 'but you must be satisfied in knowing that I admired you much more than your friend.' My dear love, I cannot believe there ever was or ever could be any thing to admire in me especially as far as sight goes – I cannot be admired, I am not a thing to be admired. You are, I love you; all I can bring you is a swooning admiration of your Beauty. I hold that place among Men which snub-nos'd brunettes with meeting eyebrows do among women – they are trash to me – unless I should find one among them with a fire in her heart like the one that burns in mine. You absorb me in spite of myself – you alone: for I look not forward with any pleasure to what is call'd being settled in the world; I tremble at domestic cares – yet for you I would meet them, though if it would leave you the happier I would rather die than do so. I have two luxuries to brood over in my walks, your Loveliness and the hour of my death. O that I could have possession of them both in the same minute. I hate the world: it batters too much the wings of my self-will, and would I could take a sweet poison from your lips to send me out of it. From no others would I take it. I am indeed astonish'd to find myself so careless of all charms but yours – remembering as I do the time when even a bit of ribband was a matter of interest with me. What softer words can I find for you after this – what it is I will not read. Nor will I say more here, but in a Postscript answer any thing else you may have mentioned in your Letter in so many words – for I am distracted with a thousand thoughts. I will imagine you Venus tonight and pray, pray, pray to your star like a Heathen.

Your's ever, fair Star,

JOHN KEATS.

My seal is mark'd like a family table cloth with my Mother's initial F for Fanny: put between my Father's initials. You will soon hear from me again. My respectful Compliments to your Mother. Tell Margaret I'll send her a reef of best rocks and tell Sam I will give him my light bay hunter if he will tie the Bishop hand and foot and pack him in a hamper and send him down for me to bathe him for his health with a Necklace of good snubby stones about his Neck.

IV.

Shanklin, Thursday Night.
[*Postmark*, Newport, 9 August, 1819.]

My dear Girl,

You say you must not have any more such Letters
as the last: I'll try that you shall not by running obstinate
the other way. Indeed I have not fair play – I am not idle
enough for proper downright love-letters – I leave this
minute a scene in our Tragedy and see you (think it not
blasphemy) through the mist of Plots, speeches, counter-
plots and counterspeeches. The Lover is madder than I
am – I am nothing to him – he has a figure like the Statue
of Meleager and double distilled fire in his heart. Thank
God for my diligence! were it not for that I should be
miserable. I encourage it, and strive not to think of you
– but when I have succeeded in doing so all day and as
far as midnight, you return, as soon as this artificial
excitement goes off, more severely from the feyer I am
left in. Upon my soul I cannot say what you could like
me for. I do not think myself a fright any more than I
do Mr. A., Mr. B., and Mr. C. – yet if I were a woman
I should not like A. B. C. But enough of this. So you
intend to hold me to my promise of seeing you in a short
time. I shall keep it with as much sorrow as gladness:
for I am not one of the Paladins of old who liv'd upon

water grass and smiles for years together. What though would I not give tonight for the gratification of my eyes alone? This day week we shall move to Winchester; for I feel the want of a Library. Brown will leave me there to pay a visit to Mr. Snook at Bedhampton: in his absence I will flit to you and back. I will stay very little while, for as I am in a train of writing now I fear to disturb it – let it have its course bad or good – in it I shall try my own strength and the public pulse. At Winchester I shall get your Letters more readily; and it being a cathedral City I shall have a pleasure always a great one to me when near a Cathedral, of reading them during the service up and down the Aisle.

Friday Morning. – Just as I had written thus far last night, Brown came down in his morning coat and nightcap, saying he had been refresh'd by a good sleep and was very hungry. I left him eating and went to bed, being too tired to enter into any discussions. You would delight very greatly in the walks about here; the Cliffs, woods, hills, sands, rocks &c. about here. They are however not so fine but I shall give them a hearty good bye to exchange them for my Cathedral. – Yet again I am not so tired of Scenery as to hate Switzerland. We might spend a pleasant year at Berne or Zurich – if it should please Venus to hear my 'Beseech thee to hear us O Goddess.' And if she should hear, God forbid we should what people call, *settle* – turn into a pond, a stagnant Lethe – a vile crescent, row or buildings. Better be imprudent moveables than prudent fixtures. Open my

Mouth at the Street door like the Lion's head at Venice to receive hateful cards, letters, messages. Go out and wither at tea parties; freeze at dinners; bake at dances; simmer at routs. No my love, trust yourself to me and I will find you nobler amusements, fortune favouring. I fear you will not receive this till Sunday or Monday: as the Irishman would write do not in the mean while hate me. I long to be off for Winchester, for I begin to dislike the very door-posts here – the names, the pebbles. You ask after my health, not telling me whether you are better. I am quite well. You going out is no proof that you are: how is it? Late hours will do you great harm. What fairing is it? I was alone for a couple of days while Brown went gadding over the country with his ancient knapsack. Now I like his society as well as any Man's, yet regretted his return – it broke in upon me like a Thunderbolt. I had got in a dream among my Books – really luxuriating in a solitude and silence you alone should have disturb'd.

Your ever affectionate

JOHN KEATS.

V.

Winchester, August 17th.

[*Postmark*, 16 August, 1819.]

My dear Girl – what shall I say for myself? I have been here four days and not yet written you – 'tis true I have had many teasing letters of business to dismiss – and I have been in the Claws, like a serpent in an Eagle's, of the last act of our Tragedy. This is no excuse; I know it; I do not presume to offer it. I have no right either to ask a speedy answer to let me know how lenient you are – I must remain some days in a Mist – I see you through a Mist: as I daresay you do me by this time. Believe in the first Letters I wrote you: I assure you I felt as I wrote – I could not write so now. The thousand images I have had pass through my brain – my uneasy spirits – my unguess'd fate – all spread as a veil between me and you. Remember I have had no idle leisure to brood over you – 'tis well perhaps I have not. I could not have endured the throng of jealousies that used to haunt me before I had plunged so deeply into imaginary interests. I would fain, as my sails are set, sail on without an interruption for a Brace of Months longer – I am in complete cue – in the fever; and shall in these four Months do an immense deal. This Page as my eye skims over it I see is excessively unloverlike and ungallant – I cannot help it – I am no officer in yawning quarters; no Parson-Romeo. My Mind is heap'd to the full; stuff'd like a cricket ball – if I strive to fill it more it would burst. I know the generality of women would hate me for this; that I should have so unsoften'd, so hard a Mind as to forget them; forget the brightest realities for the dull imaginations of my own Brain. But I conjure you to give it a fair thinking; and ask yourself whether 'tis not better to explain my feelings to you, than write artificial Passion. – Besides, you would see through it. It would be vain to strive to deceive you. 'Tis harsh, harsh, I know it. My heart seems now made of iron – I could not write a proper answer to an invitation to Idalia. You are my Judge: my forehead is on the ground. You seem offended at a little simple innocent childish playfulness in my last. I did not seriously mean to say that you were endeavouring to make me keep my promise. I beg your pardon for it. 'Tis but *just* your Pride should take the alarm – *seriously*. You say I may do as I please – I do not think with any conscience I can; my cash resources are for the present stopp'd; I fear for some time. I spend no money, but it increases my debts. I have all my life thought very little of these matters – they seem not to belong to me. It may be a proud sentence; but by Heaven I am as entirely above all matters of interest as the Sun is above the Earth – and though of my own money I should be careless; of my Friends' I must be spare. You see how I go on – like so many strokes of a hammer. I cannot help it – I am impell'd, driven to it. I am not happy enough for silken Phrases, and silver sentences. I can no more use soothing words to you than if I were at this moment engaged in a charge of Cavalry. Then you will say I should not write at all. – Should I not? This Winchester is a fine place: a beautiful Cathedral and many other ancient buildings in the Environs. The little coffin of a room at Shanklin is changed for a large room, where I can promenade at my pleasure – looks out onto a beautiful – blank side of a house. It is strange I should like it better than the view of the sea from our window at Shanklin. I began to hate the very posts there – the voice of the old Lady over the way was getting a great Plague. The Fisherman's face never altered any more than our black teapot – the knob however was knock'd off to my little relief. I am getting a great dislike of the picturesque; and can only relish it over again by seeing you enjoy it. One of the pleasantest things I have seen lately was at Cowes. The Regent in his Yatch (I think they spell it) was anchored opposite – a beautiful vessel – and all the Yatchs and boats on the coast were passing and re-passing it; and circuiting and tacking about it in every direction – I never beheld anything so silent, light, and graceful. – As we pass'd over to Southampton, there was nearly an accident. There came by a Boat well mann'd, with two naval officers at the stern. Our Bow-lines took the top of their little mast and snapped it off close by the board. Had the mast been a little stouter they would have been upset. In so trifling an event I could not help admiring our seamen – neither officer nor man in the whole Boat moved a muscle – they scarcely notic'd it even with words. Forgive me for this flint-worded Letter, and believe and see that I cannot think of you without some sort of energy – though mal à propos. Even as I leave off it seems to me that a few more moments' thought of you would uncrystallize and dissolve me. I must not give way to it – but turn to my writing again – if I fail I shall die hard. O my love, your lips are growing sweet again to my fancy – I must forget them. Ever your affectionate

KEATS.

VI.

Fleet Street, Monday Morn.

[*Postmark*, Lombard Street, 14 September, 1819.]

My dear Girl,

I have been hurried to town by a Letter from my brother George; it is not of the brightest intelligence. Am I mad or not? I came by the Friday night coach and have not yet been to Hampstead. Upon my soul it is not my fault. I cannot resolve to mix any pleasure with my days: they go one like another, undistinguishable. If I were to see you today it would destroy the half comfortable sullenness I enjoy at present into downright perplexities. I love you too much to venture to Hampstead, I feel it is not paying a visit, but venturing into a fire. *Que feraije?* as the French novel writers say in fun, and I in earnest: really what can I do? Knowing well that my life must be passed in fatigue and trouble, I have been endeavouring to wean myself from you: for to myself alone what can be much of a misery? As far as they regard myself I can despise all events: but I cannot cease to love you. This morning I scarcely know what I am doing. I am going to Walthamstow. I shall return to Winchester tomorrow; whence you shall hear from me in a few days. I am a Coward, I cannot bear the pain of being happy: 'tis out of the question: I must admit no thought of it.

Yours ever affectionately

JOHN KEATS.

VII.

[*Postmark*, 11 October, 1819.]

My sweet Girl,

I am living today in yesterday: I was in a complete fascination all day. I feel myself at your mercy. Write me ever so few lines and tell me you will never for ever be less kind to me than yesterday. – You dazzled me. There is nothing in the world so bright and delicate. When Brown came out with that seemingly true story against me last night, I felt it would be death to me if you had ever believed it – though against any one else I could muster up my obstinacy. Before I knew Brown could disprove it I was for the moment miserable. When shall we pass a day alone? I have had a thousand kisses, for which with my whole soul I thank love – but if you should deny me the thousand and first – 'twould put me to the proof how great a misery I could live through. If you should ever carry your threat yesterday into execution – believe me 'tis not my pride, my vanity or any petty passion would torment me – really 'twould hurt my heart – I could not bear it. I have seen Mrs.

Dilke this morning; she says she will come with me any fine day.

Ever yours

JOHN KEATS.

Ah hertè mine!

VIII.

25 College Street.

[*Postmark*, 13 October, 1819.]

My dearest Girl,

    This moment I have set myself to copy some verses out fair. I cannot proceed with any degree of content. I must write you a line or two and see if that will assist in dismissing you from my Mind for ever so short a time. Upon my Soul I can think of nothing else. The time is passed when I had power to advise and warn you against the unpromising morning of my Life. My love has made me selfish. I cannot exist without you. I am forgetful of everything but seeing you again – my Life seems to stop there – I see no further. You have absorb'd me. I have a sensation at the present moment as though I was dissolving – I should be exquisitely miserable without the hope of soon seeing you. I should be afraid to separate myself far from you. My sweet Fanny, will your heart never change? My love, will it? I have no limit now to my love...... Your note came in just here. I cannot be happier away from you. 'Tis richer than an Argosy of Pearles. Do not threat me even in jest. I have been astonished that Men could die Martyrs for religion – I have shudder'd at it. I shudder no more – I could be martyr'd for my Religion – Love is my religion – I could die for that. I could die for you. My Creed is Love and you are its only tenet. You have ravish'd me away by a Power I cannot resist; and yet I could resist till I saw you; and even since I have seen you I have endeavoured often 'to reason against the reasons of my Love.' I can do that no more – the pain would be too great. My love is selfish. I cannot breathe without you.

Yours for ever

JOHN KEATS.

IX.

Great Smith Street,

Tuesday Morn.

[*Postmark*, College Street, 19 October, 1819.]

My sweet Fanny,

On awakening from my three days dream ('I cry to dream again') I find one and another astonish'd at my idleness and thoughtlessness. I was miserable last night – the morning is always restorative. I must be busy, or try to be so. I have several things to speak to you of tomorrow morning. Mrs. Dilke I should think will tell you that I purpose living at Hampstead. I must impose chains upon myself. I shall be able to do nothing. I should like to cast the die for Love or death. I have no Patience with any thing else – if you ever intend to be cruel to me as you say in jest now but perhaps may sometimes be in earnest, be so now – and I will – my mind is in a tremble, I cannot tell what I am writing.

Ever my love yours

JOHN KEATS.

X–XXXII.
WENTWORTH PLACE.

X.

Dearest Fanny, I shall send this the moment you return. They say I must remain confined to this room for some time. The consciousness that you love me will make a pleasant prison of the house next to yours. You must come and see me frequently: this evening, without fail – when you must not mind about my speaking in a low tone for I am ordered to do so though I *can* speak out.

Yours ever

sweetest love. –

J. KEATS.

Perhaps your Mother is not at home and so you must wait till she comes. You must see me tonight and let me hear you promise to come tomorrow.

Brown told me you were all out. I have been looking for the stage the whole afternoon. Had I known this I could not have remain'd so silent all day.

XI.

My dearest Girl,

      If illness makes such an agreeable variety in the manner of your eyes I should wish you sometimes to be ill. I wish I had read your note before you went last night that I might have assured you how far I was from suspecting any coldness. You had a just right to be a little silent to one who speaks so plainly to you. You must believe – you shall, you will – that I can do nothing, say nothing, think nothing of you but what has its spring in the Love which has so long been my pleasure and torment. On the night I was taken ill – when so violent a rush of blood came to my Lungs that I felt nearly suffocated – I assure you I felt it possible I might not survive, and at that moment thought of nothing but you. When I said to Brown 'this is unfortunate' I thought of you. 'Tis true that since the first two or three days other subjects have entered my head. I shall be looking forward to Health and the Spring and a regular routine of our old Walks.

Your affectionate

J. K.

XII.

My sweet love, I shall wait patiently till tomorrow before I see you, and in the mean time, if there is any need of such a thing, assure you by your Beauty, that whenever I have at any time written on a certain unpleasant subject, it has been with your welfare impress'd upon my mind. How hurt I should have been had you ever acceded to what is, notwithstanding, very reasonable! How much the more do I love you from the general result! In my present state of Health I feel too much separated from you and could almost speak to you in the words of Lorenzo's Ghost to Isabella

> 'Your Beauty grows upon me and I feel
> A greater love through all my essence steal.'

My greatest torment since I have known you has been the fear of you being a little inclined to the Cressid; but that suspicion I dismiss utterly and remain happy in the surety of your Love, which I assure you is as much a wonder to me as a delight. Send me the words 'Good night' to put under my pillow.

Dearest Fanny,

Your affectionate

J. K.

XIII.

My dearest Girl,

According to all appearances I am to be separated from you as much as possible. How I shall be able to bear it, or whether it will not be worse than your presence now and then, I cannot tell. I must be patient, and in the mean time you must think of it as little as possible. Let me not longer detain you from going to Town – there may be no end to this imprisoning of you. Perhaps you had better not come before tomorrow evening: send me however without fail a good night.

You know our situation – what hope is there if I should be recovered ever so soon – my very health will not suffer me to make any great exertion. I am recommended not even to read poetry, much less write it. I wish I had even a little hope. I cannot say forget me – but I would mention that there are impossibilities in the world. No more of this. I am not strong enough to be weaned – take no notice of it in your good night.

Happen what may I shall ever be my dearest Love

Your affectionate

J. K.

XIV.

My dearest Girl, how could it ever have been my wish to forget you? how could I have said such a thing? The utmost stretch my mind has been capable of was to endeavour to forget you for your own sake seeing what a chance there was of my remaining in a precarious state of health. I would have borne it as I would bear death if fate was in that humour: but I should as soon think of choosing to die as to part from you. Believe too my Love that our friends think and speak for the best, and if their best is not our best it is not their fault. When I am better I will speak with you at large on these subjects, if there is any occasion – I think there is none. I am rather nervous today perhaps from being a little recovered and suffering my mind to take little excursions beyond the doors and windows. I take it for a good sign, but as it must not be encouraged you had better delay seeing me till tomorrow. Do not take the trouble of writing much: merely send me my good night.

Remember me to your Mother and Margaret.

Your affectionate

J. K.

XV.

My dearest Fanny,

   Then all we have to do is to be patient. What-
ever violence I may sometimes do myself by hinting at
what would appear to any one but ourselves a matter of
necessity, I do not think I could bear any approach of a
thought of losing you. I slept well last night, but cannot
say that I improve very fast. I shall expect you tomorrow,
for it is certainly better that I should see you seldom. Let
me have your good night.

                              Your affectionate

                                   J. K.

XVI.

My dearest Fanny,

    I read your note in bed last night, and that might be the reason of my sleeping so much better. I think Mr Brown is right in supposing you may stop too long with me, so very nervous as I am. Send me every evening a written Good night. If you come for a few minutes about six it may be the best time. Should you ever fancy me too low-spirited I must warn you to ascribe it to the medicine I am at present taking which is of a nerve-shaking nature. I shall impute any depression I may experience to this cause. I have been writing with a vile old pen the whole week, which is excessively ungallant. The fault is in the Quill: I have mended it and still it is very much inclin'd to make blind es. However these last lines are in a much better style of penmanship, thof a little disfigured by the smear of black currant jelly; which has made a little mark on one of the pages of Brown's Ben Jonson, the very best book he has. I have lick'd it but it remains very purple. I did not know whether to say purple or blue so in the mixture of the thought wrote purplue which may be an excellent name for a colour made up of those two, and would suit well to start next spring. Be very careful of open doors and windows and going without your duffle grey. God bless you Love!

J. KEATS.

P.S. I am sitting in the back room. Remember me to your Mother.

XVII.

My dear Fanny,

　　Do not let your mother suppose that you hurt me by writing at night. For some reason or other your last night's note was not so treasureable as former ones. I would fain that you call me *Love* still. To see you happy and in high spirits is a great consolation to me – still let me believe that you are not half so happy as my restoration would make you. I am nervous, I own, and may think myself worse than I really am; if so you must indulge me, and pamper with that sort of tenderness you have manifested towards me in different Letters. My sweet creature when I look back upon the pains and torments I have suffer'd for you from the day I left you to go to the Isle of Wight; the ecstasies in which I have pass'd some days and the miseries in their turn, I wonder the more at the Beauty which has kept up the spell so fervently. When I send this round I shall be in the front parlour watching to see you show yourself for a minute in the garden. How illness stands as a barrier betwixt me and you! Even if I was well – I must make myself as good a Philosopher as possible. Now I have had opportunities of passing nights anxious and awake I have found other thoughts intrude upon me. 'If I should die,' said I to myself, 'I have left no immortal work behind me – nothing to make my friends proud of my memory – but

I have lov'd the principle of beauty in all things, and if I had had time I would have made myself remember'd.' Thoughts like these came very feebly whilst I was in health and every pulse beat for you – now you divide with this (may *I* say it?) 'last infirmity of noble minds' all my reflection.

God bless you, Love.

J. KEATS.

XVIII.

My dearest Girl,

You spoke of having been unwell in your last note: have you recover'd? That note has been a great delight to me. I am stronger than I was: the Doctors say there is very little the matter with me, but I cannot believe them till the weight and tightness of my Chest is mitigated. I will not indulge or pain myself by complaining of my long separation from you. God alone knows whether I am destined to taste of happiness with you: at all events I myself know thus much, that I consider it no mean Happiness to have lov'd you thus far – if it is to be no further I shall not be unthankful – if I am to recover, the day of my recovery shall see me by your side from which nothing shall separate me. If well you are the only medicine that can keep me so. Perhaps, aye surely, I am writing in too depress'd a state of mind – ask your Mother to come and see me – she will bring you a better account than mine.

Ever your affectionate

JOHN KEATS.

XIX.

My dearest Girl,

   Indeed I will not deceive you with respect to my Health. This is the fact as far as I know. I have been confined three weeks and am not yet well – this proves that there is something wrong about me which my constitution will either conquer or give way to. Let us hope for the best. Do you hear the Thrush singing over the field? I think it is a sign of mild weather – so much the better for me. Like all Sinners now I am ill I philosophize, aye out of my attachment to every thing, Trees, flowers, Thrushes, Spring, Summer, Claret, &c. &c. – aye every thing but you. – My sister would be glad of my company a little longer. That Thrush is a fine fellow. I hope he was fortunate in his choice this year. Do not send any more of my Books home. I have a great pleasure in the thought of you looking on them.

Ever yours

my sweet Fanny

J. K.

XX.

My dearest Girl,

    I continue much the same as usual, I think a little better. My spirits are better also, and consequently I am more resign'd to my confinement. I dare not think of you much or write much to you. Remember me to all.

Ever your affectionate

JOHN KEATS.

XXI.

My dear Fanny,

    I think you had better not make any long stay with me when Mr. Brown is at home. Whenever he goes out you may bring your work. You will have a pleasant walk today. I shall see you pass. I shall follow you with my eyes over the Heath. Will you come towards evening instead of before dinner? When you are gone, 'tis past – if you do not come till the evening I have something to look forward to all day. Come round to my window for a moment when you have read this. Thank your Mother, for the preserves, for me. The raspberry will be too sweet not having any acid; therefore as you are so good a girl I shall make you a present of it. Good bye

My sweet Love!

J. KEATS.

XXII.

My dearest Fanny,

　　The power of your benediction is of not so weak a nature as to pass from the ring in four and twenty hours – it is like a sacred Chalice once consecrated and ever consecrate. I shall kiss your name and mine where your Lips have been – Lips! why should a poor prisoner as I am talk about such things? Thank God, though I hold them the dearest pleasures in the universe, I have a consolation independent of them in the certainty of your affection. I could write a song in the style of Tom Moore's Pathetic about Memory if that would be any relief to me. No – 'twould not. I will be as obstinate as a Robin, I will not sing in a cage. Health is my expected heaven and you are the Houri – this word I believe is both singular and plural – if only plural, never mind – you are a thousand of them.

Ever yours affectionately

my dearest,

J. K.

You had better not come to day.

XXIII.

My dearest Love,

　　You must not stop so long in the cold – I have been suspecting that window to be open. – Your note half-cured me. When I want some more oranges I will tell you – these are just à propos. I am kept from food so feel rather weak – otherwise very well. Pray do not stop so long upstairs – it makes me uneasy – come every now and then and stop a half minute. Remember me to your Mother.

Your ever affectionate

J. KEATS.

XXIV.

Sweetest Fanny,

You fear, sometimes, I do not love you so much as you wish? My dear Girl I love you ever and ever and without reserve. The more I have known the more have I lov'd. In every way – even my jealousies have been agonies of Love, in the hottest fit I ever had I would have died for you. I have vex'd you too much. But for Love! Can I help it? You are always new. The last of your kisses was ever the sweetest; the last smile the brightest; the last movement the gracefullest. When you pass'd my window home yesterday, I was fill'd with as much admiration as if I had then seen you for the first time. You uttered a half complaint once that I only lov'd your beauty. Have I nothing else then to love in you but that? Do not I see a heart naturally furnish'd with wings imprison itself with me? No ill prospect has been able to turn your thoughts a moment from me. This perhaps should be as much a subject of sorrow as joy – but I will not talk of that. Even if you did not love me I could not help an entire devotion to you: how much more deeply then must I feel for you knowing you love me. My Mind has been the most discontented and restless one that ever was put into a body too small for it. I never felt my Mind repose upon anything with complete and undistracted enjoyment – upon no person but you. When you are in the room my thoughts never fly out of window: you always concentrate my whole senses. The anxiety shown about our Loves in your last note is an immense pleasure to me: however you must not suffer such speculations to molest you any more: nor will I any more believe you can have the least pique against me. Brown is gone out – but here is Mrs. Wylie – when she is gone I shall be awake for you. – Remembrances to your Mother.

Your affectionate

J. KEATS.

XXV.

My dear Fanny,

  I am much better this morning than I was a week ago: indeed I improve a little every day. I rely upon taking a walk with you upon the first of May: in the mean time undergoing a babylonish captivity I shall not be jew enough to hang up my harp upon a willow, but rather endeavour to clear up my arrears in versifying, and with returning health begin upon something new: pursuant to which resolution it will be necessary to have my or rather Taylor's manuscript, which you, if you please, will send by my Messenger either today or tomorrow. Is Mr. D. with you today? You appeared very much fatigued last night: you must look a little brighter this morning. I shall not suffer my little girl ever to be obscured like glass breath'd upon, but always bright as it is her *nature to*. Feeding upon sham victuals and sitting by the fire will completely annul me. I have no need of an enchanted wax figure to duplicate me, for I am melting in my proper person before the fire. If you meet with anything better (worse) than common in your Magazines let me see it.

    Good bye my sweetest Girl.

        J. K.

XXVI.

My dearest Fanny, whenever you know me to be alone, come, no matter what day. Why will you go out this weather? I shall not fatigue myself with writing too much I promise you. Brown says I am getting stouter. I rest well and from last night do not remember any thing horrid in my dream, which is a capital symptom, for any organic derangement always occasions a Phantasmagoria. It will be a nice idle amusement to hunt after a motto for my Book which I will have if lucky enough to hit upon a fit one – not intending to write a preface. I fear I am too late with my note – you are gone out – you will be as cold as a topsail in a north latitude – I advise you to furl yourself and come in a doors.

Good bye Love.

J. K.

XXVII.

My dearest Fanny, I slept well last night and am no worse this morning for it. Day by day if I am not deceived I get a more unrestrain'd use of my Chest. The nearer a racer gets to the Goal the more his anxiety becomes; so I lingering upon the borders of health feel my impatience increase. Perhaps on your account I have imagined my illness more serious than it is: how horrid was the chance of slipping into the ground instead of into your arms – the difference is amazing Love. Death must come at last; Man must die, as Shallow says; but before that is my fate I fain would try what more pleasures than you have given, so sweet a creature as you can give. Let me have another opportunity of years before me and I will not die without being remember'd. Take care of yourself dear that we may both be well in the Summer. I do not at all fatigue myself with writing, having merely to put a line or two here and there, a Task which would worry a stout state of the body and mind, but which just suits me as I can do no more.

Your affectionate

J. K.

XXVIII.

My dearest Fanny,

I had a better night last night than I have had since my attack, and this morning I am the same as when you saw me. I have been turning over two volumes of Letters written between Rousseau and two Ladies in the perplexed strain of mingled finesse and sentiment in which the Ladies and gentlemen of those days were so clever, and which is still prevalent among Ladies of this Country who live in a state of reasoning romance. The likeness however only extends to the mannerism, not to the dexterity. What would Rousseau have said at seeing our little correspondence! What would his Ladies have said! I don't care much – I would sooner have Shakspeare's opinion about the matter. The common gossiping of washerwomen must be less disgusting than the continual and eternal fence and attack of Rousseau and these sublime Petticoats. One calls herself Clara and her friend Julia, two of Rousseau's heroines – they all [at] the same time christen poor Jean Jacques St. Preux – who is the pure cavalier of his famous novel. Thank God I am born in England with our own great Men before my eyes. Thank God that you are fair and can love me without being Letter-written and sentimentaliz'd into it. – Mr. Barry Cornwall has sent me another Book, his first, with a polite note. I must do what I can to make him sensible of the esteem I have for his kindness. If this north east would take a turn it would be so much the better for me. Good bye, my love, my dear love, my beauty –

love me for ever.

J. K.

XXIX.

My dearest Fanny,

Though I shall see you in so short a time I cannot forbear sending you a few lines. You say I did not give you yesterday a minute account of my health. Today I have left off the Medicine which I took to keep the pulse down and I find I can do very well without it, which is a very favourable sign, as it shows there is no inflammation remaining. You think I may be wearied at night you say: it is my best time; I am at my best about eight o'Clock. I received a Note from Mr. Procter today. He says he cannot pay me a visit this weather as he is fearful of an inflammation in the Chest. What a horrid climate this is? or what careless inhabitants it has? You are one of them. My dear girl do not make a joke of it: do not expose yourself to the cold. There's the Thrush again – I can't afford it – he'll run me up a pretty Bill for Music – besides he ought to know I deal at Clementi's. How can you bear so long an imprisonment at Hampstead? I shall always remember it with all the gusto that a monopolizing carle should. I could build an Altar to you for it.

Your affectionate

J. K.

XXX.

My dearest Girl,

As, from the last part of my note you must see how gratified I have been by your remaining at home, you might perhaps conceive that I was equally bias'd the other way by your going to Town, I cannot be easy tonight without telling you you would be wrong to suppose so. Though I am pleased with the one, I am not displeased with the other. How do I dare to write in this manner about my pleasures and displeasures? I will tho' whilst I am an invalid, in spite of you. Good night, Love!

J. K.

XXXI.

My dearest Girl,

In consequence of our company I suppose I shall not see you before tomorrow. I am much better today – indeed all I have to complain of is want of strength and a little tightness in the Chest. I envied Sam's walk with you today; which I will not do again as I may get very tired of envying. I imagine you now sitting in your new black dress which I like so much and if I were a little less selfish and more enthusiastic I should run round and surprise you with a knock at the door. I fear I am too prudent for a dying kind of Lover. Yet, there is a great difference between going off in warm blood like Romeo, and making one's exit like a frog in a frost. I had nothing particular to say today, but not intending that there shall be any interruption to our correspondence (which at some future time I propose offering to Murray) I write something. God bless you my sweet Love! Illness is a long lane, but I see you at the end of it, and shall mend my pace as well as possible.

J. K.

XXXII.

Dear Girl,

Yesterday you must have thought me worse than I really was. I assure you there was nothing but regret at being obliged to forego an embrace which has so many times been the highest gust of my Life. I would not care for health without it. Sam would not come in – I wanted merely to ask him how you were this morning. When one is not quite well we turn for relief to those we love: this is no weakness of spirit in me: you know when in health I thought of nothing but you; when I shall again be so it will be the same. Brown has been mentioning to me that some hint from Sam, last night, occasions him some uneasiness. He whispered something to you concerning Brown and old Mr. Dilke which had the complexion of being something derogatory to the former. It was connected with an anxiety about Mr. D. Sr's death and an anxiety to set out for Chichester. These sort of hints point out their own solution: one cannot pretend to a delicate ignorance on the subject: you understand the whole matter. If any one, my sweet Love, has misrepresented, to you, to your Mother or Sam, any circumstances which are at all likely, at a tenth remove, to create suspicions among people who from their own interested notions slander others, pray tell me: for I feel the least attaint on the disinterested character of Brown very deeply. Perhaps Reynolds or some other of my friends may come towards evening, therefore you may choose whether you will come to see me early today before or after dinner as you may think fit. Remember me to your Mother and tell her to drag you to me if you show the least reluctance –

[Signature cut off.]

XXXIII–XXXVII.
KENTISH TOWN – PREPARING
FOR ITALY.

XXXIII.

My dearest Girl,

I endeavour to make myself as patient as possible. Hunt amuses me very kindly – besides I have your ring on my finger and your flowers on the table. I shall not expect to see you yet because it would be so much pain to part with you again. When the Books you want come you shall have them. I am very well this afternoon. My dearest . . .

[Signature cut off.]

XXXIV.

My dearest Fanny,

For this Week past I have been employed in marking the most beautiful passages in Spenser, intending it for you, and comforting myself in being somehow occupied to give you however small a pleasure. It has lightened my time very much. I am much better. God bless you.

Your affectionate

J. KEATS.

XXXV.

My dearest Fanny,

I have been a walk this morning with a book in my hand, but as usual I have been occupied with nothing but you: I wish I could say in an agreeable manner. I am tormented day and night. They talk of my going to Italy. 'Tis certain I shall never recover if I am to be so long separate from you: yet with all this devotion to you I cannot persuade myself into any confidence of you. Past experience connected with the fact of my long separation from you gives me agonies which are scarcely to be talked of. When your mother comes I shall be very sudden and expert in asking her whether you have been to Mrs. Dilke's, for she might say no to make me easy. I am literally worn to death, which seems my only recourse. I cannot forget what has pass'd. What? nothing with a man of the world, but to me deathful. I will get rid of this as much as possible. When you were in the habit of flirting with Brown you would have left off, could your own heart have felt one half of one pang mine did. Brown is a good sort of Man – he did not know he was doing me to death by inches. I feel the effect of every one of those hours in my side now; and for that cause, though he has done me many services, though I know his love and friendship for me, though at this moment I should be without pence were it not for his assistance, I will never see or speak to him until we are both old men, if we are to be. I *will* resent my heart having been made a football. You will call this madness. I have heard you say that it was not unpleasant to wait a few years – you have amusements – your mind is away – you have not brooded over one idea as I have, and how should you? You are to me an object intensely desirable – the air I breathe in a room empty of you is unhealthy. I am not the same to you – no – you can wait – you have a thousand activities – you can be happy without me. Any party, any thing to fill up the day has been enough. How have you pass'd this month? Who have you smil'd with? All this may seem savage in me. You do not feel as I do – you do not know what it is to love – one day you may – your time is not come. Ask yourself how many unhappy hours Keats has caused you in Loneliness. For myself I have been a Martyr the whole time, and for this reason I speak; the confession is forc'd from me by the torture. I appeal to you by the blood of that Christ you believe in: Do not write to me if you have done anything this month which it would have pained me to have seen. You may have altered – if you have not – if you still behave in dancing rooms and other societies as I have seen you – I do not want to live – if you have done so I wish this coming night may be my last. I cannot live without you, and not only you but *chaste you: virtuous you*. The Sun rises and sets, the day passes, and you follow the bent of your inclination to a certain extent –

you have no conception of the quantity of miserable feeling that passes through me in a day – Be serious! Love is not a plaything – and again do not write unless you can do it with a crystal conscience. I would sooner die for want of you than——

Yours for ever

J. KEATS.

XXXVI.

My dearest Fanny,

My head is puzzled this morning, and I scarce know what I shall say though I am full of a hundred things. 'Tis certain I would rather be writing to you this morning, notwithstanding the alloy of grief in such an occupation, than enjoy any other pleasure, with health to boot, unconnected with you. Upon my soul I have loved you to the extreme. I wish you could know the Tenderness with which I continually brood over your different aspects of countenance, action and dress. I see you come down in the morning: I see you meet me at the Window – I see every thing over again eternally that I ever have seen. If I get on the pleasant clue I live in a sort of happy misery, if on the unpleasant 'tis miserable misery. You complain of my illtreating you in word, thought and deed – I am sorry, – at times I feel bitterly sorry that I ever made you unhappy – my excuse is that those words have been wrung from me by the sharpness of my feelings. At all events and in any case I have been wrong; could I believe that I did it without any cause, I should be the most sincere of Penitents. I could give way to my repentant feelings now, I could recant all my suspicions, I could mingle with you heart and Soul though absent, were it not for some parts of your Letters.

Do you suppose it possible I could ever leave you? You know what I think of myself and what of you. You know that I should feel how much it was my loss and how little yours. My friends laugh at you! I know some of them – when I know them all I shall never think of them again as friends or even acquaintance. My friends have behaved well to me in every instance but one, and there they have become tattlers, and inquisitors into my conduct; spying upon a secret I would rather die than share it with any body's confidence. For this I cannot wish them well, I care not to see any of them again. If I am the Theme, I will not be the Friend of idle Gossips. Good gods what a shame it is our Loves should be so put into the microscope of a Coterie. Their laughs should not affect you (I may perhaps give you reasons some day for these laughs, for I suspect a few people to hate me well enough, *for reasons I know of*, who have pretended a great friendship for me) when in competition with one, who if he never should see you again would make you the Saint of his memory. These Laughers, who do not like you, who envy you for your Beauty, who would have God-bless'd me from you for ever; who were plying me with disencouragements with respect to you eternally. People are revengful – do not mind them – do nothing but love me – if I knew that for certain life and health will in such event be a heaven, and death itself will be less painful. I long to believe in immortality. I shall never be able to bid you an entire farewell. If I am destined to be happy with you here – how short is the longest Life. I wish to believe in immortality – I wish to live with you for ever. Do not let my name ever pass between you and those laughers; if I have no other merit than the great Love for you, that were sufficient to keep me sacred and unmentioned in such society. If I have been cruel and unjust I swear my love has ever been greater than my cruelty which last [*sic*] but a minute whereas my Love come what will shall last for ever. If concession to me has hurt your Pride God knows I have had little pride in my heart when thinking of you. Your name never passes my Lips – do not let mine pass yours. Those People do not like me. After reading my Letter you even then wish to see me. I am strong enough to walk over – but I dare not. I shall feel so much pain in parting with you again. My dearest love, I am afraid to see you; I am strong, but not strong enough to see you. Will my arm be ever round you again, and if so shall I be obliged to leave you again? My sweet Love! I am happy whilst I believe your first Letter. Let me be but certain that you are mine heart and soul, and I could die more happily than I could otherwise live. If you think me cruel – if you think I have sleighted you – do muse it over again and see into my heart. My love to you is 'true as truth's simplicity and simpler than the infancy of truth' as I think I once said before. How could I sleight you? How threaten to leave you? not in the spirit of a Threat to you – no – but in the spirit of Wretchedness in myself. My fairest, my delicious, my angel Fanny! do not believe me such a vulgar fellow. I will be as patient in illness and as believing in Love as I am able.

Yours for ever my dearest.

JOHN KEATS.

XXXVII.

I do not write this till the last,
that no eye may catch it.

My dearest Girl,

I wish you could invent some means to make me
at all happy without you. Every hour I am more and
more concentrated in you; every thing else tastes like
chaff in my Mouth. I feel it almost impossible to go to
Italy – the fact is I cannot leave you, and shall never taste
one minute's content until it pleases chance to let me
live with you for good. But I will not go on at this rate.
A person in health as you are can have no conception
of the horrors that nerves and a temper like mine go
through. What Island do your friends propose retiring
to? I should be happy to go with you there alone, but
in company I should object to it; the backbitings and
jealousies of new colonists who have nothing else to
amuse themselves, is unbearable. Mr. Dilke came to see
me yesterday, and gave me a very great deal more pain
than pleasure. I shall never be able any more to endure
the society of any of those who used to meet at Elm
Cottage and Wentworth Place. The last two years taste
like brass upon my Palate. If I cannot live with you I will
live alone. I do not think my health will improve much
while I am separated from you. For all this I am averse

to seeing you – I cannot bear flashes of light and return into my gloom again. I am not so unhappy now as I should be if I had seen you yesterday. To be happy with you seems such an impossibility! it requires a luckier Star than mine! it will never be. I enclose a passage from one of your letters which I want you to alter a little – I want (if you will have it so) the matter express'd less coldly to me. If my health would bear it, I could write a Poem which I have in my head, which would be a consolation for people in such a situation as mine. I would show some one in Love as I am, with a person living in such Liberty as you do. Shakespeare always sums up matters in the most sovereign manner. Hamlet's heart was full of such Misery as mine is when he said to Ophelia 'Go to a Nunnery, go, go!' Indeed I should like to give up the matter at once – I should like to die. I am sickened at the brute world which you are smiling with. I hate men, and women more. I see nothing but thorns for the future – wherever I may be next winter, in Italy or nowhere, Brown will be living near you with his indecencies. I see no prospect of any rest. Suppose me in Rome – well, I should there see you as in a magic glass going to and from town at all hours, [. . .] I wish you could infuse a little confidence of human nature into my heart. I cannot muster any – the world is too brutal for me – I am glad there is such a thing as the grave – I am sure I shall never have any rest till I get there. At any rate I will indulge myself by never seeing any more Dilke or Brown or any of their Friends. I wish I was either in your arms full of faith or that a Thunder bolt would strike me.

God bless you.

J. K.

Your affectionate
J. K—

Poems

"Fanny Brawne"
from a silhouette
by Pierre Édouard

'Bright star! would I were steadfast as thou art'

Bright star! would I were steadfast as thou art –
   Not in lone splendour hung aloft the night
And watching, with eternal lids apart,
   Like nature's patient, sleepless Eremite,
The moving waters at their priestlike task
   Of pure ablution round earth's human shores,
Or gazing on the new soft-fallen mask
   Of snow upon the mountains and the moors –
No – yet still steadfast, still unchangeable,
   Pillowed upon my fair love's ripening breast,
To feel for ever its soft swell and fall,
   Awake for ever in a sweet unrest,
Still, still to hear her tender-taken breath,
And so live ever – or else swoon to death.

The Eve of St Agnes

I

St Agnes' Eve – Ah, bitter chill it was!
The owl, for all his feathers, was a-cold;
The hare limped trembling through the frozen grass,
And silent was the flock in woolly fold:
Numb were the Beadsman's fingers, while he told
His rosary, and while his frosted breath,
Like pious incense from a censer old,
Seemed taking flight for heaven, without a death,
Past the sweet Virgin's picture, while his prayer he
    saith.

II

His prayer he saith, this patient, holy man;
Then takes his lamp, and riseth from his knees,
And back returneth, meagre, barefoot, wan,
Along the chapel aisle by slow degrees:
The sculptured dead, on each side, seem to freeze,
Emprisoned in black, purgatorial rails;
Knights, ladies, praying in dumb orat'ries,
He passeth by; and his weak spirit fails
To think how they may ache in icy hoods and mails.

III

Northward he turneth through a little door,
And scarce three steps, ere Music's golden tongue
Flattered to tears this agèd man and poor;
But no – already had his deathbell rung:
The joys of all his life were said and sung:
His was harsh penance on St Agnes' Eve.
Another way he went, and soon among
Rough ashes sat he for his soul's reprieve,
And all night kept awake, for sinners' sake to grieve.

IV

That ancient Beadsman heard the prelude soft;
And so it chanced, for many a door was wide,
From hurry to and fro. Soon, up aloft,
The silver, snarling trumpets 'gan to chide:
The level chambers, ready with their pride,
Were glowing to receive a thousand guests:
The carvèd angels, ever eager-eyed,
Stared, where upon their heads the cornice rests,
With hair blown back, and wings put cross-wise on
    their breasts.

V

At length burst in the argent revelry,
With plume, tiara, and all rich array,
Numerous as shadows haunting faerily
The brain, new-stuffed, in youth, with triumphs gay
Of old romance. These let us wish away,
And turn, sole-thoughted, to one Lady there,

Whose heart had brooded, all that wintry day,
   On love, and winged St Agnes' saintly care,
As she had heard old dames full many times declare.

VI

   They told her how, upon St Agnes' Eve,
   Young virgins might have visions of delight,
   And soft adorings from their loves receive
   Upon the honeyed middle of the night,
   If ceremonies due they did aright;
   As, supperless to bed they must retire,
   And couch supine their beauties, lily white;
   Nor look behind, nor sideways, but require
Of Heaven with upward eyes for all that they desire.

VII

   Full of this whim was thoughtful Madeline:
   The music, yearning like a God in pain,
   She scarcely heard: her maiden eyes divine,
   Fixed on the floor, saw many a sweeping train
   Pass by – she heeded not at all: in vain
   Came many a tip-toe, amorous cavalier,
   And back retired – not cooled by high disdain,
   But she saw not: her heart was otherwhere.
She sighed for Agnes' dreams, the sweetest of the year.

VIII

   She danced along with vague, regardless eyes,
   Anxious her lips, her breathing quick and short:
   The hallowed hour was near at hand: she sighs

Amid the timbrels, and the thronged resort
Of whisperers in anger, or in sport;
'Mid looks of love, defiance, hate, and scorn,
Hoodwinked with faery fancy – all amort,
Save to St Agnes and her lambs unshorn,
And all the bliss to be before to-morrow morn.

IX

So, purposing each moment to retire,
She lingered still. Meantime, across the moors,
Had come young Porphyro, with heart on fire
For Madeline. Beside the portal doors,
Buttressed from moonlight, stands he, and implores
All saints to give him sight of Madeline
But for one moment in the tedious hours,
That he might gaze and worship all unseen;
Perchance speak, kneel, touch, kiss – in sooth such
    things have been.

X

He ventures in – let no buzzed whisper tell,
All eyes be muffled, or a hundred swords
Will storm his heart, Love's fev'rous citadel:
For him, those chambers held barbarian hordes,
Hyena foemen, and hot-blooded lords,
Whose very dogs would execrations howl
Against his lineage: not one breast affords
Him any mercy, in that mansion foul,
Save one old beldame, weak in body and in soul.

XI

Ah, happy chance! the agèd creature came,
Shuffling along with ivory-headed wand,
To where he stood, hid from the torch's flame,
Behind a broad hall-pillar, far beyond
The sound of merriment and chorus bland:
He startled her; but soon she knew his face,
And grasped his fingers in her palsied hand,
Saying, 'Mercy, Porphyro! hie thee from this place:
They are all here to-night, the whole blood-thirsty
    race!

XII

'Get hence! get hence! there's dwarfish Hildebrand –
He had a fever late, and in the fit
He cursèd thee and thine, both house and land:
Then there's that old Lord Maurice, not a whit
More tame for his grey hairs – Alas me! flit!
Flit like a ghost away.' 'Ah, gossip dear,
We're safe enough; here in this arm-chair sit,
And tell me how –' 'Good Saints! not here, not here;
Follow me, child, or else these stones will be thy bier.'

XIII

He followed through a lowly archèd way,
Brushing the cobwebs with his lofty plume,
And as she muttered, 'Well-a – well-a-day!'
He found him in a little moonlight room,
Pale, latticed, chill, and silent as a tomb.
'Now tell me where is Madeline,' said he,

'O tell me, Angela, by the holy loom
Which none but secret sisterhood may see,
When they St Agnes' wool are weaving piously.'

XIV

'St Agnes? Ah! it is St Agnes' Eve –
Yet men will murder upon holy days:
Thou must hold water in a witch's sieve,
And be liege-lord of all the Elves and Fays,
To venture so: it fills me with amaze
To see thee, Porphyro! – St Agnes' Eve!
God's help! my lady fair the conjuror plays
This very night. Good angels her deceive!
But let me laugh awhile, I've mickle time to grieve.'

XV

Feebly she laugheth in the languid moon,
While Porphyro upon her face doth look,
Like puzzled urchin on an agèd crone
Who keepeth closed a wondrous riddle-book,
As spectacled she sits in chimney nook.
But soon his eyes grew brilliant, when she told
His lady's purpose; and he scarce could brook
Tears, at the thought of those enchantments cold,
And Madeline asleep in lap of legends old.

XVI

Sudden a thought came like a full-blown rose,
Flushing his brow, and in his painèd heart
Made purple riot; then doth he propose

A stratagem, that makes the beldame start:
'A cruel man and impious thou art:
Sweet lady, let her pray, and sleep, and dream
Alone with her good angels, far apart
From wicked men like thee. Go, go! – I deem
Thou canst not surely be the same that thou didst
    seem.'

XVII

'I will not harm her, by all saints I swear,'
Quoth Porphyro: 'O may I ne'er find grace
When my weak voice shall whisper its last prayer,
If one of her soft ringlets I displace,
Or look with ruffian passion in her face:
Good Angela, believe me by these tears,
Or I will, even in a moment's space,
Awake, with horrid shout, my foeman's ears,
And beard them, though they be more fanged than
    wolves and bears.'

XVIII

'Ah! why wilt thou affright a feeble soul?
A poor, weak, palsy-stricken, churchyard thing,
Whose passing-bell may ere the midnight toll;
Whose prayers for thee, each morn and evening,
Were never missed.' – Thus plaining, doth she bring
A gentler speech from burning Porphyro,
So woeful, and of such deep sorrowing,
That Angela gives promise she will do
Whatever he shall wish, betide her weal or woe.

XIX

Which was, to lead him, in close secrecy,
Even to Madeline's chamber, and there hide
Him in a closet, of such privacy
That he might see her beauty unespied,
And win perhaps that night a peerless bride,
While legioned faeries paced the coverlet,
And pale enchantment held her sleepy-eyed.
Never on such a night have lovers met,
Since Merlin paid his Demon all the monstrous debt.

XX

'It shall be as thou wishest,' said the Dame:
'All cates and dainties shall be storèd there
Quickly on this feast-night; by the tambour frame
Her own lute thou wilt see. No time to spare,
For I am slow and feeble, and scarce dare
On such a catering trust my dizzy head.
Wait here, my child, with patience; kneel in prayer
The while. Ah! thou must needs the lady wed,
Or may I never leave my grave among the dead.'

XXI

So saying, she hobbled off with busy fear.
The lover's endless minutes slowly passed;
The dame returned, and whispered in his ear
To follow her; with agèd eyes aghast
From fright of dim espial. Safe at last,
Through many a dusky gallery, they gain
The maiden's chamber, silken, hushed, and chaste;

Where Porphyro took covert, pleased amain.
His poor guide hurried back with agues in her brain.

XXII

Her faltering hand upon the balustrade,
Old Angela was feeling for the stair,
When Madeline, St Agnes' charmèd maid,
Rose, like a missioned spirit, unaware:
With silver taper's light, and pious care,
She turned, and down the agèd gossip led
To a safe level matting. Now prepare,
Young Porphyro, for gazing on that bed –
She comes, she comes again, like ring-dove frayed and
    fled.

XXIII

Out went the taper as she hurried in;
Its little smoke, in pallid moonshine, died:
She closed the door, she panted, all akin
To spirits of the air, and visions wide –
No uttered syllable, or, woe betide!
But to her heart, her heart was voluble,
Paining with eloquence her balmy side;
As though a tongueless nightingale should swell
Her throat in vain, and die, heart-stiflèd, in her dell.

XXIV

A casement high and triple-arched there was,
All garlanded with carven imag'ries
Of fruits, and flowers, and bunches of knot-grass,

And diamonded with panes of quaint device,
Innumerable of stains and splendid dyes,
As are the tiger-moth's deep-damasked wings;
And in the midst, 'mong thousand heraldries,
And twilight saints, and dim emblazonings,
A shielded scutcheon blushed with blood of queens and
    kings.

XXV

Full on this casement shone the wintry moon,
And threw warm gules on Madeline's fair breast,
As down she knelt for heaven's grace and boon;
Rose-bloom fell on her hands, together pressed,
And on her silver cross soft amethyst,
And on her hair a glory, like a saint:
She seemed a splendid angel, newly dressed,
Save wings, for Heaven – Porphyro grew faint;
She knelt, so pure a thing, so free from mortal taint.

XXVI

Anon his heart revives; her vespers done,
Of all its wreathèd pearls her hair she frees;
Unclasps her warmèd jewels one by one;
Loosens her fragrant bodice; by degrees
Her rich attire creeps rustling to her knees:
Half-hidden, like a mermaid in sea-weed,
Pensive awhile she dreams awake, and sees,
In fancy, fair St Agnes in her bed,
But dares not look behind, or all the charm is fled.

XXVII

Soon, trembling in her soft and chilly nest,
In sort of wakeful swoon, perplexed she lay,
Until the poppied warmth of sleep oppressed
Her soothèd limbs, and soul fatigued away –
Flown, like a thought, until the morrow-day;
Blissfully havened both from joy and pain;
Clasped like a missal where swart Paynims pray;
Blinded alike from sunshine and from rain,
As though a rose should shut, and be a bud again.

XXVIII

Stolen to this paradise, and so entranced,
Porphyro gazed upon her empty dress,
And listened to her breathing, if it chanced
To wake into a slumbrous tenderness;
Which when he heard, that minute did he bless,
And breathed himself: then from the closet crept,
Noiseless as fear in a wide wilderness,
And over the hushed carpet, silent, stepped,
And 'tween the curtains peeped, where, lo! – how fast
    she slept.

XXIX

Then by the bed-side, where the faded moon
Made a dim, silver twilight, soft he set
A table, and, half anguished, threw thereon
A cloth of woven crimson, gold, and jet –
O for some drowsy Morphean amulet!
The boisterous, midnight, festive clarion,

The kettle-drum, and far-heard clarinet,
Affray his ears, though but in dying tone;
The hall door shuts again, and all the noise is gone.

XXX

And still she slept an azure-lidded sleep,
In blanchèd linen, smooth, and lavendered,
While he from forth the closet brought a heap
Of candied apple, quince, and plum, and gourd,
With jellies soother than the creamy curd,
And lucent syrups, tinct with cinnamon;
Manna and dates, in argosy transferred
From Fez; and spicèd dainties, every one,
From silken Samarkand to cedared Lebanon.

XXXI

These delicates he heaped with glowing hand
On golden dishes and in baskets bright
Of wreathèd silver; sumptuous they stand
In the retirèd quiet of the night,
Filling the chilly room with perfume light.
'And now, my love, my seraph fair, awake!
Thou art my heaven, and I thine eremite:
Open thine eyes, for meek St Agnes' sake,
Or I shall drowse beside thee, so my soul doth ache.'

XXXII

Thus whispering, his warm, unnervèd arm
Sank in her pillow. Shaded was her dream
By the dusk curtains – 'twas a midnight charm

Impossible to melt as icèd stream:
The lustrous salvers in the moonlight gleam;
Broad golden fringe upon the carpet lies.
It seemed he never, never could redeem
From such a steadfast spell his lady's eyes;
So mused awhile, entoiled in woofèd fantasies.

XXXIII

Awakening up, he took her hollow lute,
Tumultuous, and, in chords that tenderest be,
He played an ancient ditty, long since mute,
In Provence called, 'La belle dame sans mercy',
Close to her ear touching the melody –
Wherewith disturbed, she uttered a soft moan:
He ceased – she panted quick – and suddenly
Her blue affrayèd eyes wide open shone.
Upon his knees he sank, pale as smooth-sculptured
    stone.

XXXIV

Her eyes were open, but she still beheld,
Now wide awake, the vision of her sleep –
There was a painful change, that nigh expelled
The blisses of her dream so pure and deep.
At which fair Madeline began to weep,
And moan forth witless words with many a sigh,
While still her gaze on Porphyro would keep;
Who knelt, with joinèd hands and piteous eye,
Fearing to move or speak, she looked so dreamingly.

XXXV

'Ah, Porphyro!' said she, 'but even now
Thy voice was at sweet tremble in mine ear,
Made tuneable with every sweetest vow,
And those sad eyes were spiritual and clear:
How changed thou art! How pallid, chill, and
    drear!
Give me that voice again, my Porphyro,
Those looks immortal, those complainings dear!
O leave me not in this eternal woe,
For if thou diest, my Love, I know not where to go.'

XXXVI

Beyond a mortal man impassioned far
At these voluptuous accents, he arose,
Ethereal, flushed, and like a throbbing star
Seen mid the sapphire heaven's deep repose;
Into her dream he melted, as the rose
Blendeth its odour with the violet –
Solution sweet. Meantime the frost-wind blows
Like Love's alarum pattering the sharp sleet
Against the window-panes; St Agnes' moon hath set.

XXXVII

'Tis dark: quick pattereth the flaw-blown sleet.
'This is no dream, my bride, my Madeline!'
'Tis dark: the icèd gusts still rave and beat.
'No dream, alas! alas! and woe is mine!
Porphyro will leave me here to fade and pine. –
Cruel! what traitor could thee hither bring?

I curse not, for my heart is lost in thine,
    Though thou forsakest a deceivèd thing –
A dove forlorn and lost with sick unprunèd wing.'

XXXVIII

    'My Madeline! sweet dreamer! lovely bride!
    Say, may I be for aye thy vassal blessed?
    Thy beauty's shield, heart-shaped and vermeil
        dyed?
    Ah, silver shrine, here will I take my rest
    After so many hours of toil and quest,
    A famished pilgrim – saved by miracle.
    Though I have found, I will not rob thy nest
    Saving of thy sweet self; if thou think'st well
To trust, fair Madeline, to no rude infidel.

XXXIX

    'Hark! 'tis an elfin-storm from faery land,
    Of haggard seeming, but a boon indeed:
    Arise – arise! the morning is at hand.
    The bloated wassaillers will never heed –
    Let us away, my love, with happy speed –
    There are no ears to hear, or eyes to see,
    Drowned all in Rhenish and the sleepy mead;
    Awake! arise! my love, and fearless be,
For o'er the southern moors I have a home for thee.'

XL

She hurried at his words, beset with fears,
For there were sleeping dragons all around,
At glaring watch, perhaps, with ready spears –
Down the wide stairs a darkling way they found.
In all the house was heard no human sound.
A chain-drooped lamp was flickering by each
    door;
The arras, rich with horseman, hawk, and hound,
Fluttered in the besieging wind's uproar;
And the long carpets rose along the gusty floor.

XLI

They glide, like phantoms, into the wide hall;
Like phantoms, to the iron porch, they glide;
Where lay the Porter, in uneasy sprawl,
With a huge empty flaggon by his side:
The wakeful bloodhound rose, and shook his
    hide,
But his sagacious eye an inmate owns.
By one, and one, the bolts full easy slide –
The chains lie silent on the footworn stones –
The key turns, and the door upon its hinges groans.

XLII

And they are gone – ay, ages long ago
These lovers fled away into the storm.
That night the Baron dreamt of many a woe,
And all his warrior-guests, with shade and form
Of witch, and demon, and large coffin-worm,

Were long be-nightmared. Angela the old
Died palsy-twitched, with meagre face deform;
The Beadsman, after thousand aves told,
For aye unsought for slept among his ashes cold.

A Dream, after reading Dante's Episode of Paolo and Francesca

As Hermes once took to his feathers light,
　　When lullèd Argus, baffled, swooned and slept,
So on a Delphic reed, my idle spright
　　So played, so charmed, so conquered, so bereft
The dragon-world of all its hundred eyes;
　　And, seeing it asleep, so fled away –
Not to pure Ida with its snow-cold skies,
　　Nor unto Tempe where Jove grieved that day;
But to that second circle of sad hell,
　　Where in the gust, the whirlwind, and the flaw
Of rain and hail-stones, lovers need not tell
　　Their sorrows. Pale were the sweet lips I saw,
Pale were the lips I kissed, and fair the form
I floated with, about that melancholy storm.

La Belle Dame sans Merci. A Ballad

I

O what can ail thee, knight-at-arms,
   Alone and palely loitering?
The sedge has withered from the lake,
   And no birds sing.

II

O what can ail thee, knight-at-arms,
   So haggard and so woe-begone?
The squirrel's granary is full,
   And the harvest's done.

III

I see a lily on thy brow,
   With anguish moist and fever-dew,
And on thy cheeks a fading rose
   Fast withereth too.

IV

I met a lady in the meads,
   Full beautiful – a faery's child,
Her hair was long, her foot was light,
   And her eyes were wild.

V

I made a garland for her head,
    And bracelets too, and fragrant zone;
She looked at me as she did love,
    And made sweet moan.

VI

I set her on my pacing steed,
    And nothing else saw all day long,
For sidelong would she bend, and sing
    A faery's song.

VII

She found me roots of relish sweet,
    And honey wild, and manna-dew,
And sure in language strange she said –
    'I love thee true'.

VIII

She took me to her elfin grot,
    And there she wept and sighed full sore,
And there I shut her wild wild eyes
    With kisses four.

IX

And there she lullèd me asleep
    And there I dreamed – Ah! woe betide! –
The latest dream I ever dreamt
    On the cold hill side.

X

I saw pale kings and princes too,
　　Pale warriors, death-pale were they all;
They cried – 'La Belle Dame sans Merci
　　Thee hath in thrall!'

XI

I saw their starved lips in the gloam,
　　With horrid warning gapèd wide,
And I awoke and found me here,
　　On the cold hill's side.

XII

And this is why I sojourn here
　　Alone and palely loitering,
Though the sedge is withered from the lake,
　　And no birds sing.

Ode to Psyche

O Goddess! hear these tuneless numbers, wrung
   By sweet enforcement and remembrance dear,
And pardon that thy secrets should be sung
   Even into thine own soft-conchèd ear:
Surely I dreamt to-day, or did I see
   The wingèd Psyche with awakened eyes?
I wandered in a forest thoughtlessly,
   And, on the sudden, fainting with surprise,
Saw two fair creatures, couchèd side by side
   In deepest grass, beneath the whispering roof
   Of leaves and tremblèd blossoms, where there ran
     A brooklet, scarce espied:
'Mid hushed, cool-rooted flowers, fragrant-eyed,
   Blue, silver-white, and budded Tyrian,
They lay calm-breathing on the bedded grass;
   Their arms embraced, and their pinions too;
   Their lips touched not, but had not bade adieu,
As if disjoined by soft-handed slumber,
And ready still past kisses to outnumber
   At tender eye-dawn of aurorean love:
     The wingèd boy I knew;
But who wast thou, O happy, happy dove?
     His Psyche true!

O latest born and loveliest vision far
  Of all Olympus' faded hierarchy!
Fairer than Phoebe's sapphire-regioned star,
  Or Vesper, amorous glow-worm of the sky;
Fairer than these, though temple thou hast none,
    Nor altar heaped with flowers;
Nor virgin-choir to make delicious moan
    Upon the midnight hours;
No voice, no lute, no pipe, no incense sweet
  From chain-swung censer teeming;
No shrine, no grove, no oracle, no heat
  Of pale-mouthed prophet dreaming.

O brightest! though too late for antique vows,
  Too, too late for the fond believing lyre,
When holy were the haunted forest boughs,
  Holy the air, the water, and the fire;
Yet even in these days so far retired
  From happy pieties, thy lucent fans,
  Fluttering among the faint Olympians,
I see, and sing, by my own eyes inspired.
So let me be thy choir, and make a moan
    Upon the midnight hours;
Thy voice, thy lute, thy pipe, thy incense sweet
  From swingèd censer teeming –
Thy shrine, thy grove, thy oracle, thy heat
  Of pale-mouthed prophet dreaming.

Yes, I will be thy priest, and build a fane
   In some untrodden region of my mind,
Where branchèd thoughts, new grown with pleasant
     pain,
   Instead of pines shall murmur in the wind:
Far, far around shall those dark-clustered trees
   Fledge the wild-ridgèd mountains steep by steep;
And there by zephyrs, streams, and birds, and bees,
   The moss-lain Dryads shall be lulled to sleep;
And in the midst of this wide quietness
A rosy sanctuary will I dress
With the wreathed trellis of a working brain,
   With buds, and bells, and stars without a name,
With all the gardener Fancy e'er could feign,
   Who breeding flowers, will never breed the same:
And there shall be for thee all soft delight
   That shadowy thought can win,
A bright torch, and a casement ope at night,
   To let the warm Love in!

Ode on Melancholy

I

No, no, go not to Lethe, neither twist
   Wolf's-bane, tight-rooted, for its poisonous wine:
Nor suffer thy pale forehead to be kissed
   By nightshade, ruby grape of Proserpine;
Make not your rosary of yew-berries,
    Nor let the beetle, nor the death-moth be
      Your mournful Psyche, nor the downy owl
A partner in your sorrow's mysteries;
    For shade to shade will come too drowsily,
      And drown the wakeful anguish of the soul.

II

But when the melancholy fit shall fall
   Sudden from heaven like a weeping cloud,
That fosters the droop-headed flowers all,
   And hides the green hill in an April shroud;
Then glut thy sorrow on a morning rose,
    Or on the rainbow of the salt sand-wave,
      Or on the wealth of globèd peonies;
Or if thy mistress some rich anger shows,
    Emprison her soft hand, and let her rave,
      And feed deep, deep upon her peerless eyes.

III

She dwells with Beauty – Beauty that must die;
   And Joy, whose hand is ever at his lips
Bidding adieu; and aching Pleasure nigh,
   Turning to poison while the bee-mouth sips:
Ay, in the very temple of Delight
   Veiled Melancholy has her sovran shrine,
     Though seen of none save him whose strenuous tongue
   Can burst Joy's grape against his palate fine;
His soul shall taste the sadness of her might,
     And be among her cloudy trophies hung.

Ode on Indolence

I

One morn before me were three figures seen,
   With bowèd necks, and joinèd hands, side-faced;
And one behind the other stepped serene,
   In placid sandals, and in white robes graced;
They passed, like figures on a marble urn,
   When shifted round to see the other side;
     They came again; as when the urn once more
Is shifted round, the first seen shades return;
   And they were strange to me, as may betide
     With vases, to one deep in Phidian lore.

II

How is it, Shadows! that I knew ye not?
   How came ye muffled in so hush a masque?
Was it a silent deep-disguisèd plot
   To steal away, and leave without a task
My idle days? Ripe was the drowsy hour;
   The blissful cloud of summer-indolence
     Benumbed my eyes; my pulse grew less and less;
Pain had no sting, and pleasure's wreath no flower:
   O, why did ye not melt, and leave my sense
     Unhaunted quite of all but – nothingness?

III

A third time passed they by, and, passing, turned
  Each one the face a moment whiles to me;
Then faded, and to follow them I burned
  And ached for wings because I knew the three;
The first was a fair Maid, and Love her name;
    The second was Ambition, pale of cheek,
      And ever watchful with fatiguèd eye;
The last, whom I love more, the more of blame
    Is heaped upon her, maiden most unmeek –
      I knew to be my demon Poesy.

IV

They faded, and, forsooth! I wanted wings.
  O folly! What is love! and where is it?
And, for that poor Ambition – it springs
  From a man's little heart's short fever-fit.
For Poesy! – no, she has not a joy –
    At least for me – so sweet as drowsy noons,
      And evenings steeped in honeyed indolence.
O, for an age so sheltered from annoy,
    That I may never know how change the moons,
      Or hear the voice of busy common-sense!

V

A third time came they by – alas! wherefore?
  My sleep had been embroidered with dim dreams;
My soul had been a lawn besprinkled o'er
  With flowers, and stirring shades, and baffled
    beams:

The morn was clouded, but no shower fell,
   Though in her lids hung the sweet tears of May;
      The open casement pressed a new-leaved vine,
   Let in the budding warmth and throstle's lay;
O Shadows! 'twas a time to bid farewell!
      Upon your skirts had fallen no tears of mine.

VI

So, ye three Ghosts, adieu! Ye cannot raise
   My head cool-bedded in the flowery grass;
For I would not be dieted with praise,
   A pet-lamb in a sentimental farce!
Fade softly from my eyes, and be once more
   In masque-like figures on the dreamy urn.
      Farewell! I yet have visions for the night,
And for the day faint visions there is store.
      Vanish, ye Phantoms! from my idle sprite,
   Into the clouds, and never more return!

Lamia

PART I

Upon a time, before the faery broods
Drove Nymph and Satyr from the prosperous woods,
Before King Oberon's bright diadem,
Sceptre, and mantle, clasped with dewy gem,
Frighted away the Dryads and the Fauns
From rushes green, and brakes, and cowslipped lawns,
The ever-smitten Hermes empty left
His golden throne, bent warm on amorous theft:
From high Olympus had he stolen light,
On this side of Jove's clouds, to escape the sight
Of his great summoner, and made retreat
Into a forest on the shores of Crete.
For somewhere in that sacred island dwelt
A nymph, to whom all hoofèd Satyrs knelt,
At whose white feet the languid Tritons poured
Pearls, while on land they withered and adored.
Fast by the springs where she to bathe was wont,
And in those meads where sometime she might haunt,
Were strewn rich gifts, unknown to any Muse,
Though Fancy's casket were unlocked to choose.
Ah, what a world of love was at her feet!
So Hermes thought, and a celestial heat
Burnt from his wingèd heels to either ear,
That from a whiteness, as the lily clear,

Blushed into roses 'mid his golden hair,
Fallen in jealous curls about his shoulders bare.

From vale to vale, from wood to wood, he flew,
Breathing upon the flowers his passion new,
And wound with many a river to its head
To find where this sweet nymph prepared her secret
    bed.
In vain; the sweet nymph might nowhere be found,
And so he rested, on the lonely ground,
Pensive, and full of painful jealousies
Of the Wood-Gods, and even the very trees.
There as he stood, he heard a mournful voice,
Such as, once heard, in gentle heart destroys
All pain but pity; thus the lone voice spake:
'When from this wreathèd tomb shall I awake!
When move in a sweet body fit for life,
And love, and pleasure, and the ruddy strife
Of hearts and lips! Ah, miserable me!'
The God, dove-footed, glided silently
Round bush and tree, soft-brushing, in his speed,
The taller grasses and full-flowering weed,
Until he found a palpitating snake,
Bright, and cirque-couchant in a dusky brake.

She was a gordian shape of dazzling hue,
Vermilion-spotted, golden, green, and blue;
Striped like a zebra, freckled like a pard,
Eyed like a peacock, and all crimson barred;
And full of silver moons, that, as she breathed,

Dissolved, or brighter shone, or interwreathed
Their lustres with the gloomier tapestries –
So rainbow-sided, touched with miseries,
She seemed, at once, some penanced lady elf,
Some demon's mistress, or the demon's self.
Upon her crest she wore a wannish fire
Sprinkled with stars, like Ariadne's tiar;
Her head was serpent, but ah, bitter-sweet!
She had a woman's mouth with all its pearls complete;
And for her eyes – what could such eyes do there
But weep, and weep, that they were born so fair,
As Proserpine still weeps for her Sicilian air?
Her throat was serpent, but the words she spake
Came, as through bubbling honey, for Love's sake,
And thus – while Hermes on his pinions lay,
Like a stooped falcon ere he takes his prey –

  'Fair Hermes, crowned with feathers, fluttering light,
I had a splendid dream of thee last night:
I saw thee sitting, on a throne of gold,
Among the Gods, upon Olympus old,
The only sad one; for thou didst not hear
The soft, lute-fingered Muses chanting clear,
Nor even Apollo when he sang alone,
Deaf to his throbbing throat's long, long melodious
    moan.
I dreamt I saw thee, robed in purple flakes,
Break amorous through the clouds, as morning breaks,
And, swiftly as a bright Phoebean dart,
Strike for the Cretan isle; and here thou art!

Too gentle Hermes, hast thou found the maid?'
Whereat the star of Lethe not delayed
His rosy eloquence, and thus inquired:
'Thou smooth-lipped serpent, surely high inspired!
Thou beauteous wreath, with melancholy eyes,
Possess whatever bliss thou canst devise,
Telling me only where my nymph is fled –
Where she doth breathe!' 'Bright planet, thou hast said,'
Returned the snake, 'but seal with oaths, fair God!'
'I swear,' said Hermes, 'by my serpent rod,
And by thine eyes, and by thy starry crown!'
Light flew his earnest words, among the blossoms
    blown.
Then thus again the brilliance feminine:
'Too frail of heart! for this lost nymph of thine,
Free as the air, invisibly, she strays
About these thornless wilds; her pleasant days
She tastes unseen; unseen her nimble feet
Leave traces in the grass and flowers sweet;
From weary tendrils, and bowed branches green,
She plucks the fruit unseen, she bathes unseen;
And by my power is her beauty veiled
To keep it unaffronted, unassailed
By the love-glances of unlovely eyes
Of Satyrs, Fauns, and bleared Silenus' sighs.
Pale grew her immortality, for woe
Of all these lovers, and she grievèd so
I took compassion on her, bade her steep
Her hair in weird syrops, that would keep
Her loveliness invisible, yet free

To wander as she loves, in liberty.
Thou shalt behold her, Hermes, thou alone,
If thou wilt, as thou swearest, grant my boon!'
Then, once again, the charmèd God began
An oath, and through the serpent's ears it ran
Warm, tremulous, devout, psalterian.
Ravished, she lifted her Circean head,
Blushed a live damask, and swift-lisping said,
'I was a woman, let me have once more
A woman's shape, and charming as before.
I love a youth of Corinth – O the bliss!
Give me my woman's form, and place me where he is.
Stoop, Hermes, let me breathe upon thy brow,
And thou shalt see thy sweet nymph even now.'
The God on half-shut feathers sank serene,
She breathed upon his eyes, and swift was seen
Of both the guarded nymph near-smiling on the green.
It was no dream; or say a dream it was,
Real are the dreams of Gods, and smoothly pass
Their pleasures in a long immortal dream.
One warm, flushed moment, hovering, it might seem
Dashed by the wood-nymph's beauty, so he burned;
Then, lighting on the printless verdure, turned
To the swooned serpent, and with languid arm,
Deficate, put to proof the lithe Caducean charm.
So done, upon the nymph his eyes he bent
Full of adoring tears and blandishment,
And towards her stepped: she, like a moon in wane,
Faded before him, cowered, nor could restrain
Her fearful sobs, self-folding like a flower

That faints into itself at evening hour:
But the God fostering her chillèd hand,
She felt the warmth, her eyelids opened bland,
And, like new flowers at morning song of bees,
Bloomed, and gave up her honey to the lees.
Into the green-recessèd woods they flew;
Nor grew they pale, as mortal lovers do.

   Left to herself, the serpent now began
To change; her elfin blood in madness ran,
Her mouth foamed, and the grass, therewith besprent,
Withered at dew so sweet and virulent;
Her eyes in torture fixed, and anguish drear,
Hot, glazed, and wide, with lid-lashes all sear,
Flashed phosphor and sharp sparks, without one
     cooling tear.
The colours all inflamed throughout her train,
She writhed about, convulsed with scarlet pain:
A deep volcanian yellow took the place
Of all her milder-moonèd body's grace;
And, as the lava ravishes the mead,
Spoilt all her silver mail, and golden brede;
Made gloom of all her frecklings, streaks and bars,
Eclipsed her crescents, and licked up her stars.
So that, in moments few, she was undressed
Of all her sapphires, greens, and amethyst,
And rubious-argent; of all these bereft,
Nothing but pain and ugliness were left.
Still shone her crown; that vanished, also she
Melted and disappeared as suddenly;

And in the air, her new voice luting soft,
Cried, 'Lycius! gentle Lycius!' – Borne aloft
With the bright mists about the mountains hoar
These words dissolved: Crete's forests heard no more.

    Whither fled Lamia, now a lady bright,
A full-born beauty new and exquisite?
She fled into that valley they pass o'er
Who go to Corinth from Cenchreas' shore;
And rested at the foot of those wild hills,
The rugged founts of the Peræan rills,
And of that other ridge whose barren back
Stretches, with all its mist and cloudy rack,
South-westward to Cleone. There she stood
About a young bird's flutter from a wood,
Fair, on a sloping green of mossy tread,
By a clear pool, wherein she passionèd
To see herself escaped from so sore ills,
While her robes flaunted with the daffodils.

    Ah, happy Lycius! – for she was a maid
More beautiful than ever twisted braid,
Or sighed, or blushed, or on spring-flowered lea
Spread a green kirtle to the minstrelsy:
A virgin purest lipped, yet in the lore
Of love deep learnèd to the red heart's core;
Not one hour old, yet of sciential brain
To unperplex bliss from its neighbour pain,
Define their pettish limits, and estrange
Their points of contact, and swift counterchange;

Intrigue with the specious chaos, and dispart
Its most ambiguous atoms with sure art;
As though in Cupid's college she had spent
Sweet days a lovely graduate, still unshent,
And kept his rosy terms in idle languishment.

Why this fair creature chose so faerily
By the wayside to linger, we shall see;
But first 'tis fit to tell how she could muse
And dream, when in the serpent prison-house,
Of all she list, strange or magnificent:
How, ever, where she willed, her spirit went;
Whether to faint Elysium, or where
Down through tress-lifting waves the Nereids fair
Wind into Thetis' bower by many a pearly stair;
Or where God Bacchus drains his cups divine,
Stretched out, at ease, beneath a glutinous pine;
Or where in Pluto's gardens palatine
Mulciber's columns gleam in far piazzian line.
And sometimes into cities she would send
Her dream, with feast and rioting to blend;
And once, while among mortals dreaming thus,
She saw the young Corinthian Lycius
Charioting foremost in the envious race,
Like a young Jove with calm uneager face,
And fell into a swooning love of him.
Now on the moth-time of that evening dim
He would return that way, as well she knew,
To Corinth from the shore; for freshly blew
The eastern soft wind, and his galley now

Grated the quaystones with her brazen prow
In port Cenchreas, from Egina isle
Fresh anchored; whither he had been awhile
To sacrifice to Jove, whose temple there
Waits with high marble doors for blood and incense
    rare.
Jove heard his vows, and bettered his desire;
For by some freakful chance he made retire
From his companions, and set forth to walk,
Perhaps grown wearied of their Corinth talk:
Over the solitary hills he fared,
Thoughtless at first, but ere eve's star appeared
His fantasy was lost, where reason fades,
In the calmed twilight of Platonic shades.
Lamia beheld him coming, near, more near –
Close to her passing, in indifference drear,
His silent sandals swept the mossy green;
So neighboured to him, and yet so unseen
She stood: he passed, shut up in mysteries,
His mind wrapped like his mantle, while her eyes
Followed his steps, and her neck regal white
Turned – syllabling thus, 'Ah, Lycius bright,
And will you leave me on the hills alone?
Lycius, look back! and be some pity shown.'
He did – not with cold wonder fearingly,
But Orpheus-like at an Eurydice –
For so delicious were the words she sung,
It seemed he had loved them a whole summer long.
And soon his eyes had drunk her beauty up,
Leaving no drop in the bewildering cup,

And still the cup was full – while he, afraid
Lest she should vanish ere his lip had paid
Due adoration, thus began to adore
(Her soft look growing coy, she saw his chain so sure):
'Leave thee alone! Look back! Ah, Goddess, see
Whether my eyes can ever turn from thee!
For pity do not this sad heart belie –
Even as thou vanisheth so I shall die.
Stay! though a Naiad of the rivers, stay!
To thy far wishes will thy streams obey.
Stay! though the greenest woods be thy domain,
Alone they can drink up the morning rain:
Though a descended Pleiad, will not one
Of thine harmonious sisters keep in tune
Thy spheres, and as thy silver proxy shine?
So sweetly to these ravished ears of mine
Came thy sweet greeting, that if thou shouldst fade
Thy memory will waste me to a shade –
For pity do not melt!' – 'If I should stay,'
Said Lamia, 'here, upon this floor of clay,
And pain my steps upon these flowers too rough,
What canst thou say or do of charm enough
To dull the nice remembrance of my home?
Thou canst not ask me with thee here to roam
Over these hills and vales, where no joy is –
Empty of immortality and bliss!
Thou art a scholar, Lycius, and must know
That finer spirits cannot breathe below
In human climes, and live. Alas! poor youth,
What taste of purer air hast thou to soothe

My essence? What serener palaces,
Where I may all my many senses please,
And by mysterious sleights a hundred thirsts appease?
It cannot be – Adieu!' So said, she rose
Tip-toe with white arms spread. He, sick to lose
The amorous promise of her lone complain,
Swooned, murmuring of love, and pale with pain.
The cruel lady, without any show
Of sorrow for her tender favourite's woe,
But rather, if her eyes could brighter be,
With brighter eyes and slow amenity,
Put her new lips to his, and gave afresh
The life she had so tangled in her mesh;
And as he from one trance was wakening
Into another, she began to sing,
Happy in beauty, life, and love, and every thing,
A song of love, too sweet for earthly lyres,
While, like held breath, the stars drew in their panting
    fires.
And then she whispered in such trembling tone,
As those who, safe together met alone
For the first time through many anguished days,
Use other speech than looks; bidding him raise
His drooping head, and clear his soul of doubt,
For that she was a woman, and without
Any more subtle fluid in her veins
Than throbbing blood, and that the self-same pains
Inhabited her frail-strung heart as his.
And next she wondered how his eyes could miss
Her face so long in Corinth, where, she said,

She dwelt but half retired, and there had led
Days happy as the gold coin could invent
Without the aid of love; yet in content
Till she saw him, as once she passed him by,
Where 'gainst a column he leant thoughtfully
At Venus' temple porch, 'mid baskets heaped
Of amorous herbs and flowers, newly reaped
Late on that eve, as 'twas the night before
The Adonian feast; whereof she saw no more,
But wept alone those days, for why should she adore?
Lycius from death awoke into amaze,
To see her still, and singing so sweet lays;
Then from amaze into delight he fell
To hear her whisper woman's lore so well;
And every word she spake enticed him on
To unperplexed delight and pleasure known.
Let the mad poets say what'er they please
Of the sweets of Faeries, Peris, Goddesses,
There is not such a treat among them all,
Haunters of cavern, lake, and waterfall,
As a real woman, lineal indeed
From Pyrrha's pebbles or old Adam's seed.
Thus gentle Lamia judged, and judged aright,
That Lycius could not love in half a fright,
So threw the goddess off, and won his heart
More pleasantly by playing woman's part,
With no more awe than what her beauty gave,
That, while it smote, still guaranteed to save.
Lycius to all made eloquent reply,
Marrying to every word a twinborn sigh;

And last, pointing to Corinth, asked her sweet,
If 'twas too far that night for her soft feet.
The way was short, for Lamia's eagerness
Made, by a spell, the triple league decrease
To a few paces; not at all surmised
By blinded Lycius, so in her comprised.
They passed the city gates, he knew not how,
So noiseless, and he never thought to know.

As men talk in a dream, so Corinth all,
Throughout her palaces imperial,
And all her populous streets and temples lewd,
Muttered, like tempest in the distance brewed,
To the wide-spreaded night above her towers.
Men, women, rich and poor, in the cool hours,
Shuffled their sandals o'er the pavement white,
Companioned or alone; while many a light
Flared, here and there, from wealthy festivals,
And threw their moving shadows on the walls,
Or found them clustered in the corniced shade
Of some arched temple door, or dusky colonnade.

Muffling his face, of greeting friends in fear,
Her fingers he pressed hard, as one came near
With curled grey beard, sharp eyes, and smooth bald
    crown,
Slow-stepped, and robed in philosophic gown:
Lycius shrank closer, as they met and passed,
Into his mantle, adding wings to haste,
While hurried Lamia trembled: 'Ah,' said he,

'Why do you shudder, love, so ruefully?
Why does your tender palm dissolve in dew?' –
'I'm wearied,' said fair Lamia, 'tell me who
Is that old man? I cannot bring to mind
His features – Lycius! wherefore did you blind
Yourself from his quick eyes?' Lycius replied,
''Tis Apollonius sage, my trusty guide
And good instructor; but tonight he seems
The ghost of folly haunting my sweet dreams.'

   While yet he spake they had arrived before
A pillared porch, with lofty portal door,
Where hung a silver lamp, whose phosphor glow
Reflected in the slabbèd steps below,
Mild as a star in water; for so new,
And so unsullied was the marble hue,
So through the crystal polish, liquid fine,
Ran the dark veins, that none but feet divine
Could e'er have touched there. Sounds Aeolian
Breathed from the hinges, as the ample span
Of the wide doors disclosed a place unknown
Some time to any, but those two alone,
And a few Persian mutes, who that same year
Were seen about the markets: none knew where
They could inhabit; the most curious
Were foiled, who watched to trace them to their house
And but the flitter-wingèd verse must tell,
For truth's sake, what woe afterwards befell,
'Twould humour many a heart to leave them thus,
Shut from the busy world, of more incredulous.

PART II

Love in a hut, with water and a crust,
Is – Love, forgive us! – cinder, ashes, dust;
Love in a palace is perhaps at last
More grievous torment than a hermit's fast.
That is a doubtful tale from faery land,
Hard for the non-elect to understand.
Had Lycius lived to hand his story down,
He might have given the moral a fresh frown,
Or clenched it quite: but too short was their bliss
To breed distrust and hate, that make the soft voice
    hiss.
Besides, there, nightly, with terrific glare,
Love, jealous grown of so complete a pair,
Hovered and buzzed his wings, with fearful roar,
Above the lintel of their chamber door,
And down the passage cast a glow upon the floor.

    For all this came a ruin: side by side
They were enthronèd, in the eventide,
Upon a couch, near to a curtaining
Whose airy texture, from a golden string,
Floated into the room, and let appear
Unveiled the summer heaven, blue and clear,
Betwixt two marble shafts. There they reposed,
Where use had made it sweet, with eyelids closed,
Saving a tithe which love still open kept,
That they might see each other while they almost slept;
When from the slope side of a suburb hill,
Deafening the swallow's twitter, came a thrill

Of trumpets – Lycius started – the sounds fled,
But left a thought, a buzzing in his head.
For the first time, since first he harboured in
That purple-linèd palace of sweet sin,
Veiled, in a chariot, heralded along
By strewn flowers, torches, and a marriage song,
With other pageants: but this fair unknown
Had not a friend. So being left alone,
(Lycius was gone to summon all his kin)
And knowing surely she could never win
His foolish heart from its mad pompousness,
She set herself, high-thoughted, how to dress
The misery in fit magnificence.
She did so, but 'tis doubtful how and whence
Came, and who were her subtle servitors.
About the halls, and to and from the doors,
There was a noise of wings, till in short space
The glowing banquet-room shone with wide-archèd
          grace.
A haunting music, sole perhaps and lone
Supportress of the faery-roof, made moan
Throughout, as fearful the whole charm might fade.
Fresh carvèd cedar, mimicking a glade
Of palm and plantain, met from either side,
High in the midst, in honour of the bride;
Two palms and then two plantains, and so on,
From either side their stems branched one to one
All down the aislèd place; and beneath all
There ran a stream of lamps straight on from wall to
          wall.

So canopied, lay an untasted feast
Teeming with odours. Lamia, regal dressed,
Silently paced about, and as she went,
In pale contented sort of discontent,
Missioned her viewless servants to enrich
The fretted splendour of each nook and niche.
Between the tree-stems, marbled plain at first,
Came jasper panels; then anon, there burst
Forth creeping imagery of slighter trees,
And with the larger wove in small intricacies.
Approving all, she faded at self-will,
And shut the chamber up, close, hushed and still,
Complete and ready for the revels rude,
When dreadful guests would come to spoil her
    solitude.

    The day appeared, and all the gossip rout.
O senseless Lycius! Madman! wherefore flout
The silent-blessing fate, warm cloistered hours,
And show to common eyes these secret bowers?
The herd approached; each guest, with busy brain,
Arriving at the portal, gazed amain,
And entered marvelling – for they knew the street,
Remembered it from childhood all complete
Without a gap, yet ne'er before had seen
That royal porch, that high-built fair demense.
So in they hurried all, mazed, curious and keen –
Save one, who looked thereon with eye severe,
And with calm-planted steps walked in austere.
'Twas Apollonius: something too he laughed,

As though some knotty problem, that had daffed
His patient thought, had now begun to thaw,
And solve and melt – 'twas just as he foresaw.

He met within the murmurous vestibule
His young disciple. ' 'Tis no common rule,
Lycius,' said he, 'for uninvited guest
To force himself upon you, and infest
With an unbidden presence the bright throng
Of younger friends; yet must I do this wrong,
And you forgive me.' Lycius blushed, and led
The old man through the inner doors broad-spread;
With reconciling words and courteous mien
Turning into sweet milk the sophist's spleen.

Of wealthy lustre was the banquet-room,
Filled with pervading brilliance and perfume:
Before each lucid panel fuming stood
A censer fed with myrrh and spicèd wood,
Each by a sacred tripod held aloft,
Whose slender feet wide-swerved upon the soft
Wool-woofèd carpets; fifty wreaths of smoke
From fifty censers their light voyage took
To the high roof, still mimicked as they rose
Along the mirrored walls by twin-clouds odorous.
Twelve spherèd tables, by silk seats ensphered,
High as the level of a man's breast reared
On libbard's paws, upheld the heavy gold
Of cups and goblets, and the store thrice told
Of Ceres' horn, and, in huge vessels, wine

Come from the gloomy tun with merry shine.
Thus loaded with a feast the tables stood,
Each shrining in the midst the image of a God.

When in an antechamber every guest
Had felt the cold full sponge to pleasure pressed,
By ministering slaves, upon his hands and feet,
And fragrant oils with ceremony meet
Poured on his hair, they all moved to the feast
In white robes, and themselves in order placed
Around the silken couches, wondering
Whence all this mighty cost and blaze of wealth could
    spring.

Soft went the music the soft air along,
While fluent Greek a vowelled undersong
Kept up among the guests, discoursing low
At first, for scarcely was the wine at flow;
But when the happy vintage touched their brains,
Louder they talk, and louder come the strains
Of powerful instruments. The gorgeous dyes,
The space, the splendour of the draperies,
The roof of awful richness, nectarous cheer,
Beautiful slaves, and Lamia's self, appear,
Now, when the wine has done its rosy deed,
And every soul from human trammels freed,
No more so strange; for merry wine, sweet wine,
Will make Elysian shades not too fair, too divine.

Soon was God Bacchus at meridian height;
Flushed were their cheeks, and bright eyes double
    bright:
Garlands of every green, and every scent
From vales deflowered, or forest-trees branch-rent,
In baskets of bright osiered gold were brought
High as the handles heaped, to suit the thought
Of every guest – that each, as he did please,
Might fancy-fit his brows, silk-pillowed at his ease.

What wreath for Lamia? What for Lycius?
What for the sage, old Apollonius?
Upon her aching forehead be there hung
The leaves of willow and of adder's tongue;
And for the youth, quick, let us strip for him
The thyrsus, that his watching eyes may swim
Into forgetfulness; and, for the sage,
Let spear-grass and the spiteful thistle wage
War on his temples. Do not all charms fly
At the mere touch of cold philosophy?
There was an awful rainbow once in heaven:
We know her woof, her texture; she is given
In the dull catalogue of common things.
Philosophy will clip an Angel's wings,
Conquer all mysteries by rule and line,
Empty the haunted air, and gnomèd mine –
Unweave a rainbow, as it erewhile made
The tender-personed Lamia melt into a shade.

By her glad Lycius sitting, in chief place,
Scarce saw in all the room another face,
Till, checking his love trance, a cup he took
Full brimmed, and opposite sent forth a look
'Cross the broad table, to beseech a glance
From his old teacher's wrinkled countenance,
And pledge him. The bald-head philosopher
Had fixed his eye, without a twinkle or stir
Full on the alarmèd beauty of the bride,
Brow-beating her fair form, and troubling her sweet
    pride.
Lycius then pressed her hand, with devout touch,
As pale it lay upon the rosy couch:
'Twas icy, and the cold ran through his veins;
Then sudden it grew hot, and all the pains
Of an unnatural heat shot to his heart.
'Lamia, what means this? Wherefore dost thou start?
Know'st thou that man?' Poor Lamia answered not.
He gazed into her eyes, and not a jot
Owned they the lovelorn piteous appeal;
More, more he gazed; his human senses reel;
Some hungry spell that loveliness absorbs;
There was no recognition in those orbs.
'Lamia!' he cried – and no soft-toned reply.
The many heard, and the loud revelry
Grew hush; the stately music no more breathes;
The myrtle sickened in a thousand wreaths.
By faint degrees, voice, lute, and pleasure ceased;
A deadly silence step by step increased,
Until it seemed a horrid presence there,

And not a man but felt the terror in his hair.
'Lamia!' he shrieked; and nothing but the shriek
With its sad echo did the silence break.
'Begone, foul dream!' he cried, gazing again
In the bride's face, where now no azure vein
Wandered on fair-spaced temples; no soft bloom
Misted the cheek; no passion to illume
The deep-recessèd vision. All was blight;
Lamia, no longer fair, there sat a deadly white.
'Shut, shut those juggling eyes, thou ruthless man!
Turn them aside, wretch! or the righteous ban
Of all the Gods, whose dreadful images
Here represent their shadowy presences,
May pierce them on the sudden with the thorn
Of painful blindness; leaving thee forlorn,
In trembling dotage to the feeblest fright
Of conscience, for their long offended might,
For all thine impious proud-heart sophistries,
Unlawful magic, and enticing lies.
Corinthians! look upon that grey-beard wretch!
Mark how, possessed, his lashless eyelids stretch
Around his demon eyes! Corinthians, see!
My sweet bride withers at their potency.'
'Fool!' said the sophist, in an undertone
Gruff with contempt; which a death-nighing moan
From Lycius answered, as heart-struck and lost,
He sank supine beside the aching ghost.
'Fool! Fool!' repeated he, while his eyes still
Relented not, nor moved: 'From every ill
Of life have I preserved thee to this day,

And shall I see thee made a serpent's prey?'
Then Lamia breathed death-breath; the sophist's eye,
Like a sharp spear, went through her utterly,
Keen, cruel, perceant, stinging: she, as well
As her weak hand could any meaning tell,
Motioned him to be silent; vainly so,
He looked and looked again a level – *No!*
'A Serpent!' echoed he; no sooner said,
Than with a frightful scream she vanishèd:
And Lycius' arms were empty of delight,
As were his limbs of life, from that same night.
On the high couch he lay! – his friends came round –
Supported him – no pulse, or breath they found,
And, in its marriage robe, the heavy body wound.

'The day is gone, and all its sweets are gone!'

The day is gone, and all its sweets are gone!
   Sweet voice, sweet lips, soft hand, and softer breast,
Warm breath, light whisper, tender semi-tone,
   Bright eyes, accomplished shape, and languorous
      waist!
Faded the flower and all its budded charms,
   Faded the sight of beauty from my eyes,
Faded the shape of beauty from my arms,
   Faded the voice, warmth, whiteness, paradise –
Vanished unseasonably at shut of eve,
   When the dusk holiday – or holinight –
Of fragrant-curtained love begins to weave
   The woof of darkness thick, for hid delight;
But, as I've read love's missal through today,
He'll let me sleep, seeing I fast and pray.

What can I do to drive away

What can I do to drive away
Remembrance from my eyes? for they have seen,
Ay, an hour ago, my brilliant Queen!
Touch has a memory. O say, love, say,
What can I do to kill it and be free
In my old liberty?
When every fair one that I saw was fair,
Enough to catch me in but half a snare,
Not keep me there;
When, howe'er poor or parti-coloured things,
My muse had wings,
And ever ready was to take her course
Whither I bent her force,
Unintellectual, yet divine to me –
Divine, I say! What sea-bird o'er the sea
Is a philosopher the while he goes
Winging along where the great water throes?

How shall I do
To get anew
Those moulted feathers, and so mount once more
Above, above
The reach of fluttering Love,
And make him cower lowly while I soar?
Shall I gulp wine? No, that is vulgarism,

A heresy and schism,
  Foisted into the canon law of love;
No – wine is only sweet to happy men;
  More dismal cares
  Seize on me unawares –
Where shall I learn to get my peace again?
To banish thoughts of that most hateful land,
Dungeoner of my friends, that wicked strand
Where they were wrecked and live a wreckèd life;
That monstrous region, whose dull rivers pour,
Ever from their sordid urns into the shore,
Unowned of any weedy-hairèd gods;
Whose winds, all zephyrless, hold scourging rods,
Iced in the great lakes, to afflict mankind;
Whose rank-grown forests, frosted, black, and blind,
Would fright a Dryad; whose harsh-herbaged meads
Make lean and lank the starved ox while he feeds;
There flowers have no scent, birds no sweet song,
And great unerring Nature once seems wrong.

O, for some sunny spell
To dissipate the shadows of this hell!
Say they are gone – with the new dawning light
Steps forth my lady bright!
O, let me once more rest
My soul upon that dazzling breast!
Let once again these aching arms be placed,
The tender gaolers of thy waist!
And let me feel that warm breath here and there
To spread a rapture in my very hair –

O, the sweetness of the pain!
Give me those lips again!
Enough! Enough! It is enough for me
To dream of thee!

'I cry your mercy, pity, love – ay, love!'

I cry your mercy, pity, love – ay, love!
    Merciful love that tantalizes not,
One-thoughted, never-wandering, guileless love,
    Unmasked, and being seen – without a blot!
O! let me have thee whole, – all, all, be mine!
    That shape, that fairness, that sweet minor zest
Of love, your kiss – those hands, those eyes divine,
    That warm, white, lucent, million-pleasured breast –
Yourself – your soul – in pity give me all,
    Withhold no atom's atom or I die;
Or living on perhaps, your wretched thrall,
    Forget, in the mist of idle misery,
Life's purposes – the palate of my mind
Losing its gust, and my ambition blind!

To Fanny

I

Physician Nature! let my spirit blood!
　　O ease my heart of verse and let me rest;
Throw me upon thy tripod till the flood
　　Of stifling numbers ebbs from my full breast.
A theme! a theme! Great Nature! give a theme;
　　　Let me begin my dream.
I come – I see thee, as thou standest there,
Beckon me out into the wintry air.

II

Ah! dearest love, sweet home of all my fears,
　　And hopes, and joys, and panting miseries,
Tonight, if I may guess, thy beauty wears
　　　A smile of such delight,
　　　As brilliant and as bright,
　　As when with ravished, aching, vassal eyes,
　　　Lost in a soft amaze,
　　　I gaze, I gaze!

III

Who now, with greedy looks, eats up my feast?
　　What stare outfaces now my silver moon!
Ah! keep that hand unravished at the least;
　　　Let, let, the amorous burn –

But, prithee, do not turn
  The current of your heart from me so soon.
    O save, in charity,
    The quickest pulse for me!

IV

Save it for me, sweet love! though music breathe
  Voluptuous visions into the warm air,
Though swimming through the dance's dangerous
    wreath,
    Be like an April day,
    Smiling and cold and gay,
  A temperate lily, temperate as fair;
    Then, Heaven! there will be
    A warmer June for me.

V

Why, this – you'll say, my Fanny! – is not true:
  Put your soft hand upon your snowy side,
Where the heart beats; confess – 'tis nothing new –
    Must not a woman be
    A feather on the sea,
  Swayed to and fro by every wind and tide?
    Of as uncertain speed
    As blow-ball from the mead?

VI

I know it – and to know it is despair
  To one who loves you as I love, sweet Fanny!
Whose heart goes fluttering for you everywhere,

Nor, when away you roam,
Dare keep its wretched home.
Love, Love alone, has pains severe and many:
Then, loveliest! keep me free
From torturing jealousy.

VII

Ah! if you prize my subdued soul above
The poor, the fading, brief, pride of an hour,
Let none profane my Holy See of Love,
Or with a rude hand break
The sacramental cake;
Let none else touch the just new-budded flower;
If not – may my eyes close,
Love! on their last repose.

'This living hand, now warm and capable'

This living hand, now warm and capable
Of earnest grasping, would, if it were cold
And in the icy silence of the tomb,
So haunt thy days and chill thy dreaming nights
That thou would wish thine own heart dry of blood
So in my veins red life might stream again,
And thou be conscience-calmed – see here it is –
I hold it towards you.

Index of Titles

Index of First Lines